MARGUERITE PATTEN'S

Holiday COOKING

A Guide to Self-catering at Home and Abroad

COLLINS
GLASGOW AND LONDON

First published 1980
William Collins Sons and Company, Glasgow and London
© Marguerite Patten 1980
Printed in Great Britain
ISBN 0 00 411224 5

CONTENTS

INTRODUCTION

All over the world today one hears about 'self-catering'. Alluring advertisements outline the pleasures of renting villas, flats, boats and barges, caravans and tents both at home and abroad. Even some holiday camps give you the choice of catering for yourself, if you prefer to do this.

Just why is this happening? Self-catering has always been available, but never has it been so popular. One can explain it by the rising cost of hotel accommodation, which can sometimes mean that any kind of holiday is impossible, unless you are prepared to look after yourselves. Often self-catering means the difference between a rather ordinary vacation and one in an exciting part of the world.

Cost is one consideration, but there are others.

Self-catering is an ideal arrangement when you have children. They can follow a fairly normal routine, and have similar menus to those they enjoy at home. Obviously one likes to encourage children to eat new foods, but many are conservative, and parents are less likely to be worried about feeding problems if catering is done in the temporary 'home'.

If you cater for yourself it gives you a splendid opportunity to learn about the specialist foods of the area or country. It is surprising how many interesting foods are to be found in different parts of Britain, and certainly markets and food shops in other European countries are fascinating. If you consider shopping in a foreign market or in food shops as part of the holiday, I am sure you will find it enjoyable. Incidentally, it is a splendid opportunity for children to extend their vocabulary of foreign words in a practical fashion.

Many establishments offer excellent fare, but all too often hotels throughout the world serve so-called 'international' dishes for the tourist and these can mean over-popular or even dull food, which has little connection with the area. You will be able to have really cosmopolitan meals if you shop cleverly and discover where the 'locals' do their shopping; these are the shops where you are likely to find economical and interesting foods.

Generally when one considers advantages there automatically have to be disadvantages too. The obvious drawback about self-catering is that someone has to do the work – and all too often it is the person who usually provides the meals at home. The objective of this book is to give you all the help possible to make the holiday a *true* holiday for whoever is doing the major part of the cooking.

You will find advice on equipment, in case you have to provide some of your own, or even in case you are equipping a villa or caravan to let to other people. There is a chapter that highlights the specialities of various parts of Britain and other popular holiday countries. The bulk of the book though gives practical recipes that are enjoyable, a change and simple to prepare, cook and serve.

Perhaps you imagine that this is a book based upon the *theory* of self-catering. If you do, then you are quite wrong! Every year for the past few years I have spent time catering for myself and my husband, friends and family on holiday. At first I was not at all sure whether it was an experience that I would want to repeat, but I found out that if you approach the matter in a practical fashion, self-catering can be a most pleasurable and relaxing experience.

I sincerely hope that you too will find it so, and that the advice given in this book will prove of value and help.

Marguerite Patten

MAKING PREPARATIONS

Careful planning before you set off will pay huge dividends in terms of enjoying yourself at the other end. Think about what your family really needs – not what you feel you should take. It is a bit sad to take cans of baked beans to an area where exotic vegetables are cheap and plentiful. And why pack an unwieldy mouli-légumes if you know your family hates soup when the weather is hot?

Find out as much as you can about the area where you intend to stay, especially if you are going to a country you have not visited before. If you booked your holiday through a travel agency, it will be able to help you. The tourist office for the relevant country will also have lots of useful information.

Of course cost is an important part of any planning. For example it is pointless to pack foods that will cost less abroad than they do here. However, in some countries such basics as tea and coffee are expensive, so it would be worthwhile taking these. If you are travelling by air, though, do be ruthless as regards what is 'essential'. You may find yourself paying more on excess baggage than for the commodities at your destination.

THE FAMILY NEEDS

Each family varies in its needs, but certain basics are common to all of us.

If you have small children, take enough supplies of canned or powdered milk, and cans or jars of baby food, to last at least two or three days. The foods available for small children vary in different countries. Taking even a small supply will give you time to look around and shop wisely.

If members of your family are diabetic or need a special diet, do take enough of their essential foods.

Will there be food ready for you when you arrive? Some owners of rented accommodation stock up refrigerators for their visitors, but I have learned from bitter experience that 'stocking up' is rather a loose term, and may mean the basis of several good meals or a woefully meagre supply of food. Unless you are quite certain there will be plenty of ingredients which can be used for a meal without a great deal of effort (remember you will probably all be weary from travelling), it is wise to take with you one or two cans of meat, a loaf of bread and some cheese.

Finally, even if you do take a good supply of the family's favourites, remember part of the enjoyment of a self-catering holiday lies in the buying and cooking of new and exciting food.

MAKING LIFE EASY

When planning your holiday, spend some time considering ways in which you can save yourself hard work in the preparation of food.

I always take with me some polythene roaster bags and foil. These keep baking tins clean, help to produce deliciously moist meat and fish, and above all save time and effort when washing up. Foil is also very useful for covering food in the refrigerator.

You will find I mention 'wrapping in foil' in a number of recipes. If you are adapting any of your own recipes for cooking meats and other foods in the oven, remember that if you use foil you need to add about five to ten minutes' extra cooking time for each hour that you normally cook the food in an uncovered tin. Remember, too, to open the foil towards the end of the cooking time if you need to brown the food. When using roaster bags there is no need to allow additional cooking time.

I also take lots of absorbent kitchen paper. This can be used for jobs as diverse as draining salads, drying up dishes and dusting! Paper goods generally are expensive in many countries, so if you are travelling by car, pack lots in among your luggage.

If you have room, it is worthwhile taking one or two good saucepans, especially if you have to heat milk and other foods for small children. A non-stick pan is particularly useful, as it is easier to wash up. People sometimes do not look after equipment when they rent accommodation, and you do not want to start your holiday by scouring semi-clean pans. I have a saucepan which doubles as a casserole and therefore has several uses. Because it is flameproof, it can be used on the hob, under the grill and in the oven. Saucepans can be used as containers for small items of food when you are travelling.

If you have bought new equipment for your holiday, unpack it and wash off labels, etc, so that it is ready for use.

You will make cooking when you arrive easier if you try out new recipes before you go on holiday. You will find that the ingredients in the recipes may vary in different countries, but the basic ideas – meals without cooking, quick meals, easy meals, cook-and-serve-in-one-dish meals – are all devised with self-catering holidays in mind.

PLAN AHEAD

The following three pages are devoted to 'kitchen' checklists. If this is the first time you have gone on this type of holiday, you may be a little worried about what lies ahead. With good planning, you can relax, knowing you have done everything possible to make the holiday enjoyable.

If certain ingredients, like Worcestershire sauce or British mustard (which is quite unlike Continental varieties), are really essential to your family, then transfer small quantities to suitable tightly-sealed polythene containers or protect the glass containers carefully.

On the following pages I give suggestions for initial preparations: basic checklists for the camper who is carrying everything on his back and for the family travelling by car or air, as well as suggestions for food to take for the settling-in period. Travel brochures and books may indicate foods that are excessively expensive in each country, but make certain the information concerns today's situation and not yesterday's.

Take with you one or two of your favourite kitchen tools. You will be lost without a small, very sharp knife and a bread knife, so it is best not to chance being without these.

A screwdriver may sound an unlikely item, but I have found it invaluable. Plug tops and screws on saucepan handles become loose easily, and, with a screwdriver, take only minutes to put right.

If you are taking an electric kettle or iron, make sure the voltage of the place in which you are staying is compatible.

Basic Checklists

Naturally, these lists will vary according to individual needs, but the following suggestions cover most of the basics.

Food and equipment for the camper carrying everything on his back

Kitchen equipment: washing-up liquid and cloth; small portable camping gas ring; small saucepan (see comments on page 13); kettle (if space); sharp knife; bread knife; can-opener combined with bottle-opener and/or corkscrew; cup or mug; plates; personal cutlery

Food: milk powder; coffee; tea; sugar; salt; pepper; tube of mustard; packet soups (these can be used as sauces to add to meats); instant potato; dried or canned vegetables; canned stewing steak and corned beef; small pack of smoked bacon; small can of sardines; crispbread (easier than bread to carry); small amount of cheese and butter (take processed cheese or put the cheese and butter into polythene boxes); breakfast cereal (transfer this from the box to a polythene bag, securely tied); fresh fruit (apples and oranges are the easiest to carry).

This list would enable you to eat reasonably well for a couple of days while you are travelling. Don't weigh yourself down with cans out of fear that you may have to fall back on locusts and wild honey. There is almost always a local shop!

Equipment for the car traveller

Any items of bedding, etc, not listed in the inventory.

Cutlery: any you feel is essential, including a sharp knife, can-opener combined with bottle-opener and corkscrew and bread knife

Saucepan and/or frying pan
Foil and roaster bags
Absorbent kitchen paper
Washing-up liquid and disposable cloth
A few polythene food containers (select the type that stack
    together for easy transport)
Large vacuum flask
Plastic mugs
Salt, pepper, a tube of mustard

Equipment for the air traveller
A good sharp knife
Small saucepan
Can-opener combined with bottle-opener and corkscrew
Bread knife
Anything else you will need which you know or suspect will not
    be provided

Food and drink to take when travelling by car
This list covers food for the first night's and the following day's
meals so you have time to settle in.

Beverages:
Milk (dried or long-life in sealed cartons), coffee, tea, orange juice
    (in cartons or bottles), drinks for the adults.

Food:
Butter and cheese (carried in a vacuum flask or cold box)
Bread and/or crispbread
Bacon, in vacuum-sealed pack
Eggs
Good-sized cooked chicken or joints (freeze the cooked chicken in
    advance and keep it cold when travelling)
Salad ingredients (in sealed polythene container)
Meat for the next day
Soups (canned or packet)
Preserves and pickles, if desired
Sugar, salt, pepper and mustard
Cakes, biscuits or other teatime goodies
Breakfast cereals; fresh fruit

Food and drink to take when travelling by air
Your carrying capacity will be restricted unless you are prepared
to pay for excess baggage, in which case refer to the list which is
given on page 11. If, however, you are sure that food will be
waiting for you; I would advise taking only the following items
which I consider essentials:
Tea and coffee for the whole holiday, safely packed (these items
    are expensive in most countries)
Small amount of sugar to last until you can shop
Dried milk (many Continental countries have sterilized milk
    which is an acquired taste)
Crispbread
Processed cheese (instead of butter which is too soft to pack)
Vacuum pack of bacon
Dehydrated or concentrated orange juice (very expensive abroad
    and important for children) – dilute with still (as opposed to
    sparkling) mineral water if the fresh water supply is suspect.
A final tip: keep the little containers of salt and pepper usually
    provided on the flight. These will be useful until you can shop.

Ordering food in advance
It is sometimes possible to send an order for food in advance, to
be waiting for you on your arrival. Check up on this facility when
booking your holiday as it is well worth doing.

EQUIPMENT YOU WILL NEED

Of course your choice of equipment for cooking and storing food will depend very largely on the type of holiday you have chosen.

THE CAMPING HOLIDAY

For instance, on a walking holiday you will be carrying all the equipment, including the tent, on your back, and this will limit the amount you can take.

The most suitable cooker to carry is a small one with just one ring. The fuel for this, butane or propane, is easily available. You will also need a lightweight kettle and saucepans. A saucepan with separate compartments provides the facility of cooking different foods at the same time, and is ideal.

If you are travelling by car, you will be able to carry a larger tent. This, in turn, means you can have a two-burner cooker with a grill, which can be erected easily and quickly. Camping stores carry a good selection of cookers.

Some of the very large tents are almost like miniature houses, and in these you can have cookers with ovens, similar to those installed in caravans. This type of cooker is usually supplied with a special stand or table so that it remains secure and is at a comfortable height. Fuel for these cookers is provided by a gas cylinder.

Other aids to easy cooking under canvas are a pressure cooker, which is of great value when you have limited space; and a small camping refrigerator or ice-box. Tips for keeping food without a refrigerator are given on page 21.

Safety First under Canvas

The comments made regarding safety in caravans (page 17) and boats (page 19) also apply to living in tents. In addition, equipment will probably be low down and easily knocked over. So in the confined area of a tent all cooking should be done with great care. It is a good idea to cook near the entrance to the tent, but make sure you protect the cooker from high winds.

THE CARAVAN HOLIDAY

In order to provide appetizing meals on holiday you need a certain amount of equipment. I have approached the question of the equipment required in the following ways:

a. For the new owner equipping a caravan for his own use, and also to hire it out to other people.
b. For the holiday-maker renting a caravan.

Equipping a Caravan

Deal with the most important item first -- the cooker. This may be standard equipment, already installed in the caravan, but if not, then choose wisely, taking into consideration your particular needs and the space available. The cooker will be connected to a gas cylinder, and will give satisfactory results.

If you have a touring caravan, equipment must not be too heavy. Because of limited space you may find you can have only a hob with two to four burners and a grill compartment, which may be adequate for your needs. However, before you make your final decision, consider the advantages of also fitting in an oven, for this would enable you to plan complete meals and leave food cooking without attention. If there is no space under the hob unit for the oven, it could be situated elsewhere in the caravan.

If your caravan is large and on a permanent site, you will probably have adequate space for a complete cooker – even a standard-sized model. This will give the unrestricted cooking capacity to which you are accustomed at home.

Do remember that, whatever type of cooker you choose, it must be placed so it has the maximum ventilation.

A refrigerator, however small, is a great asset, especially if you intend to travel in hot weather. Caravan experts will tell you that, when touring, a refrigerator can be a problem due to the movement of the van, but I think it is worthwhile trying to find a suitable model. You can have one that runs from the gas cylinder, but remember you *must* extinguish the pilot light when you fill up the car with petrol. Alternatively, select a model that can be used on a battery or by electricity. Consult an expert about the best type for your caravan, and also about installing it; gas refrigerators must have flue vents, and all refrigerators will work satisfactorily only if they have adequate ventilation.

In large caravans there is generally no problem of space for a refrigerator. Mobile homes, as large caravans are frequently described, often have both gas and electricity, so you will have a larger selection of refrigerators from which to choose. Choose the largest size possible, and check that there will be adequate air space around it. If the caravan is being transported to a hot climate, make absolutely sure the model is of a type that will cope with the continual heat.

If you are equipping the caravan for your own use it is wise to consider non-stick saucepans and a frying pan as these save work when washing up. However, as they need careful use and cleaning, they are not really a wise purchase if you are allowing other people to use your caravan. So often the non-stick (silicone) finish is ruined by whisking or stirring food in these pans with metal utensils, or using steel wool when washing up. Holiday-makers to whom you hire your caravan may not use this type of utensil at home and could spoil them through inexperience.

Flameproof saucepans that can double as casseroles are useful items, and a pressure cooker is a very good idea (for more details, see page 37). You also need a kettle, which should be a large size if your caravan has no water-heater. You will need several knives for cutting bread, meat and chopping. Also equip the caravan with a chopping board, so that working surfaces are not spoiled.

Buy dual-purpose equipment such as a mixing bowl that would do duty as a salad bowl, casseroles with lids that can also be used for cooking, and saucepans that can double as casseroles. Space is restricted in caravans, so select equipment that stacks together, such as plastic containers for storing food. You will need one or two wooden spoons, a fish slice, a large strainer which will double as a sieve, a whisk — the small, inexpensive balloon-type is excellent, a can-opener, bottle-opener, corkscrew and grater. One or two flat baking trays are also useful for heating foods.

It is possible to choose tableware of a design that stacks easily. Shops selling caravan equipment usually offer the best selection. Check whether the design is easily and inexpensively replaced in the event of accidents. Caravan cutlery is generally attractive and quite cheap.

Unless you intend doing a lot of cooking you should not need scales — you will find on page 33 that I have given some useful homely measures for most foods. A measuring jug will be more useful than scales.

The less important cooking equipment, such as rolling pin, cake tins and pie dishes, cannot be considered as essential, but only the caravan user can decide whether their particular menus will require these. It is surprising how clever one can be at making one utensil do the work of several. Empty milk or beer bottles are good rolling-pins; a cake can be cooked in a casserole. You will find references to how cooking times vary according to the equipment used on page 22.

Other items needed are a washing-up bowl to go into the sink and a rubbish bucket; buy liners for this so that waste is wrapped up hygienically.

Renting a Caravan

If you are renting a caravan, it may be possible to see the inventory which will give you a good idea of what you need to take with you. Most caravans that are hired out are equipped with cooking equipment, cutlery, tableware, blankets and pillows.

I suggest you take your favourite sharp knife for preparing salads, fruit and vegetables, slicing meats, etc, for nothing is worse, or more dangerous than to try and carry out these various processes with a blunt knife. I already mentioned taking a saucepan-cum-casserole on page 9 and this is a wise precaution in case those supplied are not suitable, or not particularly well cared for. If you read through the list of requirements suggested above for equipping the caravan kitchen, you will be able to see what seems to be missing in the official inventory, and decide whether you need these things.

Most people do not supply dish-cloths (buy the disposable type), tea towels (often absorbent paper can be used) or steel wool for cleaning pans. It is wise to buy these, but do not use steel wool on non-stick utensils.

If you wipe greasy containers and plates before trying to wash them, you save excess grease going down the sink. If this does seem greasy, soda and boiling water work wonders.

Safety First in a Caravan

The restricted space in a caravan makes safety first of paramount importance.

Make sure a fire extinguisher is installed, and read the instructions carefully so you know exactly what to do in an emergency.

Check for any possible causes of fire. Curtains hanging near cooker hobs should be secured carefully. If you are fitting out the caravan yourself, choose a non-inflammable roller blind rather than curtains. When cooking, make sure that saucepan handles are turned inwards. In the limited space of a caravan, it is all too easy to knock against the handles when moving through the kitchen area and tip the pan over.

Deep frying is not advisable in a caravan, due to smell and the restricted space, but if you do deep fry, watch the pan *all the time*.

The gas cylinder is quite safe providing you use it carefully. Make absolutely certain that all connections are tight, and the correct gas regulator is used. When gas is in use, put the cylinder outside the caravan, and when you leave the van, turn off the gas *at the bottle*. Check the hose from the gas cylinder regularly to see there are no breaks. It is wise to carry a spare hose when touring, or at least to check if supplies are available on a site.

If the caravan has electricity never try to use appliances on plugs that are too highly loaded. Make quite sure everything has the correct plug tops fitted, and is of the correct voltage. If you use an iron in the caravan, *never* leave it switched on, and when you have finished with it, put it in a safe place while it cools down.

If the caravan is equipped with a toilet, shower or bath from the main water supply, always be certain when leaving the van that the supply is securely turned off, as great damage can be caused if flooding occurs.

On page 20 you will find a brief note about gas detectors. These are an invaluable asset in a caravan.

The normal precautions of care with cigarettes, checking on where matches are put and keeping dangerous medicines out of reach of children are even more important in the confined space of a caravan than at home.

VILLAS, FLATS AND COTTAGES

It always sounds much more luxurious to be staying in a permanent home rather than a caravan or boat, but do not be too disappointed if the cooking equipment is not as lavish as you would wish. After a day or so you will find you can adapt your usual routine. The more elaborate your own kitchen and cooking equipment, the more difficult you may feel it will be to cope in a more spartan kitchen. However, if you plan ahead and take with you the food and equipment outlined on pages 10–12, you will find that you will soon be able to cope quite adequately.

As you will appreciate, different countries not only have foods unlike our own, but also different utensils. For example, in some Continental countries you may find a shortage of ovenproof casseroles in the cupboard. This is because many Continentals use the type of saucepan that doubles up as a casserole, a very sensible and labour-saving utensil that is now becoming more popular in Britain. In this type of saucepan you can fry the meat and other ingredients on the top of the cooker, add the liquid etc, cover the pan, then put it into the oven. You have one instead of two utensils to clean, and the flavour of the fat or meat is retained.

You may find there is no grill with a Continental cooker, which means foods that you normally grill must be fried or baked.

You will achieve almost the same effect as grilling if you place the food on greased, flat baking trays in a pre-heated *very hot* oven. Unless there is a toaster supplied, you will have to forego breakfast toast. But foreign bread, rolls and croissants are invariably so interesting, that this is no great hardship.

Unless you are given a list of the foods that will be available on your arrival, assume that nothing is supplied, or that there will be only a few basics. So take at least enough convenience foods for your first evening meal and breakfast the next day. This will give you the opportunity to settle in before you go shopping.

THE BOATING HOLIDAY

The kitchen, or to be correct the galley, on even a small boat is generally an object lesson on using available space wisely. Cooking facilities are generally good, but fairly limited, unless you have a large yacht.

If you are equipping the boat yourself, the comments regarding caravans on pages 14–17 may prove interesting and helpful. It is, however, rather more important to select pots, pans and china that stack well, for reasons of safety as well as space. If equipment is securely packed, it is more likely to stay secure in bad weather.

When thinking ahead about the dishes you will cook while cruising, consider the fact that you may well have a day or so of rough, stormy weather. Plan a few simple, easy-to-digest dishes that virtually cook themselves. It is extremely difficult and uncomfortable to stand over a cooker when the boat is rolling, and could be dangerous if pans of hot food lurched off the hob.

Your choice of dishes will depend largely upon how often you will be touching land to stock up on fresh foods. Many of the recipes in this book are based upon convenience foods that you can carry with you, but there are also plenty of other suitable ideas that use fresh produce.

If you are cruising canals on a hired barge, you can tie up frequently and shop at your leisure, so meals can be quite elaborate.

Naturally the final choice of dishes will depend upon the countries in which you are travelling, and the weather you can expect.

Safety on Boats

The galley of a boat is a confined space, so it is essential to take every possible precaution to make sure accidents cannot happen.

Safety precautions in a caravan (see page 17) are also very relevant for boats.

There is an additional hazard which must be considered most carefully, and that is the possible danger of gas from the cylinder leaking into the bilges, or below deck. To prevent this, check the hose, the regulator, and all the connections from the gas cylinder most carefully. When hiring a boat or barge this will doubtless be done for you; it is, however, worth checking yourself before you attempt to light a cooker, gas refrigerator, or water heater.

A gas detector is a sensible item to have on board. Details are given below.

Consider carefully the timing of cooking meals on boats. The safest time to cook is when the boat is tied up. On a moving narrow boat, for instance, a bump against the bank could cause trouble. However, it may not always be convenient to anchor in time for a meal. In such cases, prepare fairly simple dishes, and avoid frying. Never leave the galley during the cooking period. It is also a good idea to keep other people away from the immediate vicinity of the cooker and galley when dishing up hot food, as a sudden lurch of the boat could cause an accident.

Gas Detectors

These enable you to ascertain if there is a gas leak, and are obtainable from ships' chandlers, or places specializing in boat and caravan equipment.

If you are equipping a boat or caravan to let, a gas detector is invaluable, as hirers may not always check carefully for gas faults.

HINTS TO HELP

Your holiday home may be equipped with fewer 'mod cons' than you are used to! This chapter suggests how to cope with no refrigerator, a different cooker, and bottled gas!

PERISHABLE FOODS AND HOW TO STORE THEM

Do not try to store a great variety of perishable foods if you do not have a refrigerator or ice box. You run the risk of food deteriorating and becoming harmful to health. It is much wiser, and safer, to carry canned and dried foods.

There are, however, ways of keeping many basic types of perishables fresh.

Milk should be stood in a bowl of cold water. Cover the bottle or carton with damp muslin and allow the muslin ends to soak in the water. As an alternative to fresh milk you can, of course, buy skimmed or full-cream dried milk, or cartons of long-life milk. Sterilized milk keeps better than fresh milk, but has a distinctive flavour which some people dislike. Cans of unsweetened evaporated milk, or sweetened condensed milk can be diluted with water to take the place of fresh milk.

Butter and other fats can be put into wide-necked vacuum flasks, and kept in a cool place. Unsalted butter does not keep as well as salted butter. Special coolers for both milk and butter can be bought from camping stores.

Do not try to store fresh fish and meat without a refrigerator, but cured bacon can be stored if it is kept in a cool place.

Buy small quantities only of fruit and vegetables, and allow good air circulation around them. The best way to store lettuce and similar green vegetables *without* a refrigerator is to put them, unwashed, into a tightly covered saucepan and stand it in a cool place.

Most cheeses keep well without a refrigerator, although Camembert, Brie and similar cheeses ripen very quickly in hot weather, so buy small quantities only.

Insulated Containers

Insulated cold boxes, and bags which keep iced and cold foods really fresh and cool for some hours are a great asset when transporting food. They are particularly efficient if you chill the small container enclosed with many of these for some hours in the freezing compartment of your refrigerator. You can, of course, pack a hot meal in these too. Obviously you cannot carry hot and cold dishes or drinks in the same container unless they are both insulated in separate vacuum flasks.

ADAPTING COOKING TIMES

When using unfamiliar cooking equipment, you may find you need to adapt your normal cooking times. The following points may prove helpful.

The deeper the container, the longer the cooking time. If you bake a cake or pudding in a deeper tin or dish than the one you normally use, then allow extra cooking time. I find that for each 2·5cm (1in) that the container is smaller in diameter and deeper in capacity, I must increase the cooking time by about 20 minutes. It may be necessary to reduce the temperature slightly towards the end of the cooking period, so the outside of the cake or pudding does not become too brown before the middle is cooked. If the container is wider in diameter and shallower than your usual tin or dish, reduce the cooking time by the same amount. Alternatively, you may be able to cook at a slightly hotter temperature. If you bake in a glass or china casserole, rather than a cake tin, you may also find the cooking time needs to be a little longer. This is a rough guide only, but it proves to be fairly reliable.

Pressure cookers are ideal for saving time and producing complete meals from one pan, but you have to adjust the cooking time when compared with conventional cooking methods. You will find a brief note about pressure cooking on page 37.

COOKING WITH BOTTLED GAS

The flame produced by bottled gas should be perfectly efficient. However, some types of bottled gas tend to give a flame that blackens the outside of cooking pots; this happens especially if the flame is so high that it comes up the sides of the pot. Keeping the heat well regulated, with a low or steady flame, will minimize this effect.

THE JOURNEY

The journey to your holiday destination may be a long trip which will mean meals en route.

If you are travelling by car, you can of course eat in cafés and restaurants, but you may prefer to avoid them. If you are travelling at the weekend or in the peak of the holiday season, stopping places are often crowded.

It is often more relaxing to find a pleasant place in which to stop and eat a packed meal, particularly if the weather is good. You can enjoy the fresh air and the opportunity to stretch your legs. Parking and picnic spots are not difficult to find, even when you travel on main roads, often there are designated picnic areas.

If you are travelling long distances by train it is wise to have food with you. Although you can check in advance to see what catering facilities are offered, you may find in the event that they have been cancelled or modified! It is very worrying to be with young children and find you cannot obtain even a soft drink for them.

On the next few pages are ideas for simple foods that pack well, do not dry out in transit and yet are interesting enough to make the journey a special part of the holiday period.

In addition to the suggestions given on these pages, you will find the picnic suggestions later in the book helpful too.

Golden rules when travelling are to avoid over-rich dishes, particularly if you are not a good traveller. Do not plan over-sweet things either, as they make you very thirsty. Simple, easily digested foods are the best to pack.

PLANNING THE MENU

The foods that follow are designed for family meals, so there is something for the children, as well as the adults.

Remember to have refreshing drinks as well as plenty of food. Insulated boxes or bags, and vacuum flasks, keep these at the desired temperature.

Consider the personal likes and dislikes of various members of the family if possible, and plan accordingly. For instance, some people have genuine headaches if they miss their cup of tea at a certain time.

Meal Starters

The following four simple and refreshing starters can be put into wide-necked vacuum flasks, polythene boxes or screw-topped jars. For more elaborate hors d'oeuvre, see pages 109–111.

Melon and Lemon

Dice ripe melon and sprinkle with a little lemon syrup, made by mixing diluted lemon juice with a little sugar. (This saves carrying sugar for the people who like melon sweetened.) For a more refreshing taste omit the sugar from the diluted lemon juice. The small amount of liquid makes the melon more moist. A little ginger flavour could be added too, if desired. Melon blends well with other diced fruits.

Tomato and Orange Cocktail

Canned or bottled tomato juice is much more interesting if a little fresh orange juice is added. Use about three parts tomato juice to one part orange juice.

Apple and Cheese Slices

Select 4 good-sized firm dessert apples. Blend 100g (4oz) cottage or cream cheese with a few chopped nuts, sultanas or chopped dates and a squeeze of lemon juice. Cut each apple into 4 slices and sandwich together with the cheese mixture. Separate the slices to eat this satisfying meal-starter. *Serves 4.*

Orange and Grapefruit Cocktail

Put segments of fresh or canned orange and grapefruit into containers.
Freezing: All the dishes are better freshly prepared.

Main Dishes

These should be simple, as time will be precious when you have so much to do. Fried or grilled chicken portions or lamb cutlets with salad are quickly prepared and easy to eat. Take paper napkins so that you can eat the food barbecue style, rather than with cutlery. Take also some fresh bread, butter, an assortment of cheeses, and some tomatoes and apples, for a satisfying meal.

A savoury egg flan or quiche makes another sustaining main course. The recipe opposite is for a slightly unusual quiche, but it is sufficiently firm to travel well. Make the pastry as described in the recipe below, or use a pastry mix or frozen pastry to save time. A generous quantity of pastry has been allowed in the recipe for curried quiche, as this makes it firmer for travelling, but it could be reduced slightly if you prefer a thinner crust.

Sausage and Tomato Slice

This will be a favourite with children who enjoy sausage rolls. The filling is a little more moist than when using sausagemeat alone.

Make shortcrust pastry with 225g (8oz) flour, pinch salt, 110g (4oz) fat and water to mix. The metric conversion is different from usual to give the right proportions.

Sift the flour and salt together, rub in the fat and bind with water. Roll out to an oblong shape.

Blend 225g (8oz) sausagemeat with 2 skinned and chopped tomatoes and spread over half the pastry. Moisten the edges of the pastry with a little water. Fold the plain pastry over the sausagemeat and seal the edges very firmly. Lift on to a baking tray or into a foil dish. Bake in the centre of a hot oven, 220°C, 425°F, Gas Mark 7, for 10 minutes, or until slightly browned, then lower the heat to moderate, 190°C, 375°F, Gas Mark 5 for a further 25–30 minutes. *Serves 4.*
To vary: Add approximately 50g (2oz) fried chopped mushrooms

and 1 tablespoon chopped chives and/or parsley.
Freezing: This freezes well for up to 3 months. If it is more convenient, you can freeze the home-made uncooked pastry for up to 3 months. Defrost and make the slice.

Curried Quiche

350g (12oz) shortcrust pastry
   mix or frozen shortcrust pastry
For the filling

1 medium onion	3 eggs, beaten
100g (4oz) bacon (with rinds)	150ml (¼ pint) yoghourt
100g (4oz) mushrooms	1 tablespoon tomato purée
25g (1oz) butter	salt and pepper
2–3 teaspoons curry powder	

Make up the pastry if using the mix, or allow frozen pastry to defrost sufficiently to roll out. Line a large shallow flan tin or the lid of a casserole with the pastry; place a round of foil over pastry, and then put a few crusts of bread on top to prevent the pastry from rising. Bake in a moderately hot oven, 200°C, 400°F, Gas Mark 6, for 15 minutes. Remove foil and crusts.

Peel and slice the onion, de-rind and chop the bacon, wash and slice the mushrooms. Melt the butter and cook the vegetables and bacon for several minutes; discard the bacon rinds. Blend the curry powder, eggs, yoghourt, tomato purée and a little salt and pepper with the bacon and vegetables in the pan, stir well, then spoon into the pastry case. The baking time will depend upon the depth of filling, but if you have cooked the pastry in a shallow dish, about 20–23cm (8–9in), you will need to bake it for about 25 minutes in the centre of a moderate oven, 190°C, 375°F, Gas Mark 5, or leave until set. Lower the heat slightly if the top of the filling gets rather brown. *Serves 4–6.*
To vary: Use other meat, such as diced cooked beef or corned beef, instead of bacon.
Make pastry with 225g (8oz) flour, 110g (4oz) fat etc as described for Sausage and Tomato Slice (see opposite).

Especially for Vegetarians

The following three dishes are ideal for vegetarians, and have the advantage of being pleasantly moist when eaten cold. They blend well with most salads, particularly a coleslaw (shredded white cabbage with a good dressing).

Egg and Cheese Cutlets

Hard-boil, shell and chop 4 eggs; grate 50g (2oz) Cheddar or other cheese. Make a thick white sauce with 25g (1oz) butter or margarine, 25g (1oz) flour and just 150ml (¼ pint) milk. Add the eggs and cheese, with a little salt and pepper; chopped chives or other herbs give good added flavour.

Allow the mixture to cool and form into 8 small cutlet shapes. Coat in a little seasoned flour, beaten egg and crisp breadcrumbs. Fry in hot fat until crisp and brown on both sides, then drain well on absorbent paper before cooling and packing. *Serves 4.*

To vary: Add 2–3 tablespoons soft wholemeal crumbs to the egg and cheese mixture for a firmer texture.

Macaroni Cutlets

Eating cold macaroni sounds unusual, but these cutlets are extremely good. If your family likes macaroni cheese, make some for supper one day and cook extra for this dish.

Cook 75g (3oz) short-cut macaroni in boiling salted water, then drain well. Blend with a cheese sauce made with 25g (1oz) butter or margarine, 25g (1oz) flour, and 225ml (scant ½ pint) milk. Add salt, pepper and a little made mustard when the sauce has thickened, together with 175g (6oz) grated cheese.

Allow to become quite cold and firm, then form into cutlets, coat and fry as for Egg and Cheese Cutlets (see above). *Serves 4.*

Traditional Quiche

Line the tin or dish with pastry, adding foil and crusts as for Curried Quiche on page 27. Bake in a moderately hot oven, 200°C, 400°F, Gas Mark 6 for 15 minutes. Beat 3 eggs, add 300ml (½ pint) hot milk, 175g (6oz) grated cheese and 100g (4oz) cooked sliced mushrooms or other cooked vegetables. Spoon into the hot pastry case, lower the heat to very moderate, 160°C, 325°F, Gas Mark 3 and cook for about 30 minutes, or until set. *Serves 4–6.*

Freezing: This freezes well for 3 months.

Refreshing Drinks

These are ideal for a journey or to enjoy on your holiday. When pouring lightly-iced drinks into a vacuum flask, make sure that any pieces of ice are completely crushed, as ice cubes can break the lining of some flasks. (Check with the maker's instructions.)

Lemonade

The old-fashioned method of making lemonade is quick, easy and very refreshing. Cut 2 lemons into halves and remove any pips. Put the fruit into a jug or strong container and add 600ml (1 pint) boiling water, and sugar to taste (not too much — it should be pleasantly tart). Press hard with a wooden spoon to extract as much flavour as possible. Cover and leave to cool. Strain and chill. You may find you can dilute this with quite a lot of water or soda water for a less strong beverage.

Iced Coffee

This delicious cold drink is often forgotten. The best way to combine strong coffee with a generous amount of milk is to make the coffee rather stronger than usual, cool the liquid, then pour it into ice trays and place them in the freezing compartment of the refrigerator, or the freezer. When you are ready to make the coffee, drop several coffee ice cubes into chilled milk. You may not be able to carry these solid ice cubes in your vacuum flask (see the comment at the top of the page), but you could crush and blend them with the milk.

Iced Tea

This is a very refreshing and interesting non-alcoholic cold drink. Personally, I prefer well-strained China tea, but fairly weak Indian tea could be used. Make the tea in the usual way, allow to infuse for a few minutes only, strain carefully and cool. You may like to put a few bruised mint leaves in with the tea as it cools, or a strip of top lemon zest. Make sure you use the yellow part only, as the white pith makes it bitter. When cold, add a little lemon juice; do this gradually and taste as you do so. Serve with crushed ice cubes and no milk.

WEIGHTS, MEASURES AND TEMPERATURES

When shopping abroad you will find goods are sold in metric measurements of weight, length and liquid (mass) amounts. Although we are beginning to use these in Britain, they are not sufficiently common for everyone to be familiar with the way in which they compare with Imperial measurements. The tables and information in this chapter should help you to understand how metrication affects quantities, and make shopping and cooking easier, when you have a self-catering holiday abroad. I also give a few handy measures on page 33.

WEIGHT

The metric weight for foods is calculated in kilogrammes. One kilogramme is equivalent to 2·2lb (or nearly 2¼lb). This means that when you try to assess the relevant prices in the shops, you must consider just how much more in weight you have in a kilogramme (generally shown as a kg) than an Imperial pound. Instead of ounces, the metric measurement of weight is a gramme.

In Britain we assume that 25g is equivalent to 1oz, but the accurate conversion is 28·35g. The following table will show you how weights are calculated in recipes. As you will see, adjustments have to be made from time to time, (e.g. 6oz = 175g), to compensate for the fact that 25g is not really as much as 1oz and therefore, when dealing with larger quantities, there will be too little food in metric terms unless you adjust the conversion.

ounces	actual grammes	accepted grammes	ounces	actual grammes	accepted grammes
1	28·35	25	9	255·15	250
2	56·7	50	10	283·5	275
3	85·05	75	11	311·85	300
4	113·4	100	12	340·2	350
5	141·75	125 or 150	13	368·55	375
6	170·1	175	14	396·90	400
7	198·45	200	15	425·25	425
8	226·8	225	16	453·60	450

As the tables show, 1lb (16oz) is given as 450g. In some recipes in this book you will find this as 0·5kg. I have used the less accurate conversion when you would be asking for half a kilo in shops, and the small extra quantity of food does not matter.

LIQUIDS

The basic measure for liquids is calculated in litres. One litre (1l) is equivalent to 1·76 pints (or 1¾ pints) or 35 fluid ounces (fl oz). Often recipes give the equivalent of a litre as being 2 pints, but this is not quite accurate.

There are various terms used to denote fractions of a litre. They are:

decilitres (dl) – 10 to 1 litre
centilitres (cl) – 100 to 1 litre (almost unknown in Britain, but very usual in some Continental countries for milk, beer, etc)
millilitres (ml) – 1000 to 1 litre (the measurement most commonly used in Britain, but less familiar on the Continent)
The figures below will help you when shopping for milk, etc.

pints and fluid ounces	accurate and accepted litres	accurate and accepted dl	accurate and accepted cl	accurate and accepted ml
2 (40fl oz)	1·136 (nearly 1¼l)	11·36 (12)	113·6 (120)	1136 (1200)
1 (20fl oz)	·568 (good ½l)	5·68 (6)	56·8 (60)	568 (600)
¾ (15fl oz)	·426 (scant ½l)	4·26 (4·5)	42·6 (45)	426 (450)
½ (10fl oz)	·284 (good ¼l)	2·84 (3)	28·4 (30)	284 (300)
¼ (5fl oz)	·142 (good ⅛l)	1·42 (1.5)	14·2 (15)	142 (150)
1fl oz	·0246 (2×15ml spoons)	·246 (·25)	2·46 (2·5)	24·6 (25)

You will see that in the last line above a 15ml spoon is mentioned. This is the metric spoon measure which approximates to a tablespoon. In fact it is slightly smaller, about the same size as a tablespoon in the United States. 5floz in Imperial measures is ¼ pint or approximately 8 tablespoons or 10 × 15ml spoons or American tablespoons.

An Imperial teaspoon is given as a 5ml spoon in metric measures.

As the metric tablespoons and teaspoons are so similar to our Imperial measures, we have not complicated matters by mentioning them in the actual recipes in this book.

MEASUREMENTS OF LENGTH

It is doubtful whether you will be measuring many articles used in cookery while on holiday. It is not vital to know how long a French loaf or a German sausage is! But if you are doing a lot of baking, here are a few useful points to remember. If your holiday kitchen has different-sized tins or dishes from your usual ones, then the cooking time of your recipes will differ.

If you spread the mixture over a larger area you have less depth, it takes a shorter time for the heat to penetrate, and the cooking time will be shorter.

If, on the other hand, you use a smaller container, the cooking time will be longer. In this case, it is a good idea to reduce the oven setting slightly, so that the surface of the dish does not become over-browned before the inside is completely cooked.

The metric measurement of length is a metre, and most cooking utensils will be marked in centimetres (cm). An inch is considerably longer than a centimetre, as the following table shows.

inches	actual centimetres	accepted centimetres	inches	actual centimetres	accepted centimetres
1	2·54	2·5	7	17·78	18
2	5·08	5	8	20·32	20
3	7·62	8	9	22·86	23
4	10·16	10	10	25·40	25
5	12·70	13	11	27·94	28
6	15·24	15	12	30·48	30·5

Travelling to the Shops

The comparison between kilometres and miles should not affect your cooking! But you obviously need to consider distances, with the resulting time and money spent on fares or petrol, when deciding upon how and where you will shop. A kilometre (1000 metres) is considerably shorter than a mile. A kilometre (km) is 3280·89 feet (1093·63 yards) or nearly ⅝ths of a mile. To make a quick calculation, divide the number of kilometres shown by 8 and multiply by 5. For example, 8 kilometres is about 5 miles.

HANDY MEASURES

In some recipes it is important to calculate the exact weight of ingredients. If you find there are no scales, then use a measure.

An *average* teacup holds 142ml (given as 150ml) or ¼ pint (5floz).

An *average* breakfast cup holds just twice as much, 284ml (given as 300ml) or ½ pint (10floz) – not to be confused with a United States cup measure, which is 8floz!

Unfortunately, it is not easy to judge whether the cups provided are smaller or bigger than average, so it is worth buying a measure.

The amounts below are on an accurate 284ml (300ml)/½ pint (10floz) cup measure, and the spoon measures as a standard 1 × 15ml spoon (1 tablespoon).

Breadcrumbs – soft
25g/1oz = 5 tablespoons   65g/2½oz = 1 cup
Dried fruit
25g/1oz = 2½ tablespoons   200g/7oz = 1 cup
Fats
25g/1oz = 1⅔ tablespoons   275g/10oz = 1 cup
It is, however, easier to mark the block of fat into portions. A Continental block is 0·25kg (250g/9oz).
Flour, cocoa, cornflour
25g/1oz = 3 tablespoons   150g/5oz = 1 cup
100g/4oz = 4/5ths cup   225g/8oz = 1 3/5ths cup
Golden syrup, jam, etc
25g/1oz = 1 tablespoon   425g/15oz (roughly 1lb) = 1 cup

Grated cheese – Cheddar etc
25g/1oz = 3 tablespoons   150g/5oz = 1 cup
Rice – dry, uncooked
25g/1oz = 1⅔ tablespoons   250g/9oz (helping for 6) = 1 cup
Sugar – caster or granulated
25g/1oz = 1⅔ tablespoons   275g/10oz = 1 cup
100g/4oz = 2/5ths cup   225g/8oz = 4/5ths cup
            (nearly ½ cup)

Note: All spoon measures are level.
          Cup measures are *without* pressing the food down hard.

USING THE COOKER

It always takes time to get used to a new cooker. The following information will, I hope, provide helpful short cuts.

First, the oven temperatures:

You may have a gas cooker at home, and be provided with an electric cooker – or vice versa. You will soon get used to the differences, but it is important to appreciate just how settings compare, also how positions in the oven help to determine the speed of cooking.

In Britain all new electric cookers have the temperature in degrees Celsius (°C), rather than degrees Fahrenheit (°F).

The tables opposite give both temperatures. In addition, the comparable gas setting is given, together with a description of the oven temperature. The last column tells how you can gauge the heat by a simple test or tests, if your holiday cooker has no regulator or thermostat or thermometer. These tests will also help if you have been provided with an oil or solid fuel cooker.

Fairly thick writing paper provides a good method of testing – thin paper is *not* suitable. If you have no suitable paper, a 'hand' test is also given. If using thick paper, put it into the *centre* of the oven. Watch carefully to see how soon the paper turns golden or brown to assess the approximate temperature of the oven. If you use the hand test, take great care not to touch any part of the oven.

The accurate Celsius degrees are given with the usual electric cooker setting in brackets.

Oven description	°C	°F	Gas mark	Tests
Very cool	93 (90)	200	0	a) Paper turns golden after 12 minutes b) Hand can be kept in oven without discomfort
Very cool	107 (110)	225	¼	a) Paper turns golden after 10 minutes b) Hand can be kept in oven without discomfort
Very cool	121 (120)	250	½	a) Paper turns golden after 8 minutes b) Hand can be kept in oven without discomfort
Low or cool	135 (140)	275	1	a) Paper turns golden after 6 minutes b) Hand feels pleasantly warm
Low or cool	149 (150)	300	2	a) Paper turns golden after 5 minutes b) Hand feels pleasantly warm
Very moderate	163 (160)	325	3	a) Paper turns golden brown after 2 minutes b) Hand begins to feel hot
Moderate	177 (180)	350	4	a) Paper turns golden brown after 1½ minutes b) Not comfortable for hand
Moderate	190 (190)	375	5	a) Paper turns golden brown after 1 minute b) Hand feels hot the moment it goes in

Moderately hot	204 (200)	400	6	a) Paper turns golden at once
				b) Hand held near door feels hot at once
Hot	218 (220)	425	7	a) Paper turns brown almost at once
				b) Hand held near door feels hot at once
Very hot	232 (230)	450	8	a) Blast of hot air on opening door. Do not put paper in, it will burn
				b) Uncomfortable to hold hand near oven
Very hot	246 (240)	475	9	Impossible to put hand very near the oven

The position in the oven where the food is placed is important. In most electric ovens, the top of the oven is the hottest, near the bottom of the oven the next hottest, and the centre is the coolest position. If by chance the electric oven is fan-heated, all parts of the oven are the same heat. You will recognize this oven by the sound of the fan.

In a gas cooker the top is the hottest and the farther away from the top of the oven the cooler the temperature. The floor of a gas oven is appreciably cooler than the top.

If you are using a solid fuel cooker, you will probably have two ovens – the top one hotter, giving a range of temperature from moderate to hot, the lower one cooler and ideal for slow cooking.

If you have an oil cooker it may well have a heat control as given in the table above. If not, then test carefully with paper, or your hand. The heat is regulated by the control of the wick or wicks.

In many Continental style cookers there appears to be no grill. Actually this may well be in the top of the oven and it will probably also be used for pre-heating the oven. If you have used this oven-grill for cooking food, do allow it to become quite cool before attempting to cook rather delicate cakes – should you decide these are part of you holiday menu! In the United States and Canada the grill is referred to as the broiler.

On top of an electric cooker you will have boiling plates – these may be of a solid type, in which case you will cook faster with solid based pans. If they are of the spiral type, known as radiant plates, lighter pans give quicker heating. If you are not used to electric cooking, you will find that the solid plates tend to retain heat for a longer period than a gas ring. It is therefore wise to lower the heat just *before* foods are boiling rapidly, or you may have difficulty in simmering well. With radiant plates you get a more immediate response.

If you are using gas boiling rings, take care that the heat is not too high. It should not come round the sides of the saucepan, or the food could burn.

If your holiday home has a solid fuel cooker you will have been supplied with the solid type of pans that are suitable for this. To achieve gentle simmering, you generally need to pull the pans towards the edge of the hotplate.

With an oil cooker, the heat of the burners is controlled by the height of the wicks. If you are using this type of cooker, keep the burners well cleaned and it will repay you with a lack of smoke or fumes.

USING A PRESSURE COOKER

If you have decided to use a pressure cooker, make sure that you have perfect control over the boiling ring or plate. It is essential to be able to bring the cooker to pressure over a high heat, then to reduce the heat and maintain the pressure. Sometimes caravan and camping cookers do not give this ready control.

If you are unfamiliar with a pressure cooker, read all the manufacturer's instructions carefully before using. It is important to remember that the cooking times given are from the moment the cooker reaches pressure. Here are some examples.

A beef stew takes about 15 minutes; a lamb stew about 12 minutes; minced beef only 5–6 minutes. Pot roasting of beef takes 9–10 minutes per 450g (1lb); lamb or veal 10–12 minutes; pork 13–15 minutes and chicken 5 minutes.

SELF-CATERING ABROAD

So many countries have now become popular for self-catering holidays. You will find it helpful if you acquire a little knowledge about the kind of food shops you will visit while you are away.

This section of the book deals with shopping and cooking in some of the most popular holiday countries, where self-catering is an established tradition. Obviously the information regarding each country must be general: different regions of the country will have certain specialities for you to buy and use.

All countries have a traditional cuisine, and I have given a selection of dishes from each country which can be made easily with the foods available. All are simple and quick to prepare, for however dedicated a cook you may be, I am sure that relaxation will be more important to you than slaving over a hot, foreign stove.

There is something very exciting about visiting, shopping and cooking in a new country, for there is so much to see and to compare with life at home.

If you are in a wine-producing country (there are many countries that do produce wines apart from France, Italy and Spain) do try the wines of your region. The cheaper varieties are often excellent – especially when drunk on their home ground.

It is also worth trying local wine vinegar and olive oil. Olive oil does vary considerably. If you find a good, fruity 'virgin' oil, it is worth bringing some home. Try, too, vegetables and fruit you may not use at home or do not buy because they are a luxury.

WHY MENTION FREEZING?

Many recipes have freezing notes after them. These are included in case you are travelling by car, on a fairly short journey, to a house where you will have a freezer or a refrigerator with a good-sized freezing compartment. If you are, you can extend your planning and cash in on this valuable asset. To transport your frozen, home-cooked dishes, use a cold box or bag, or wrap the containers in thick layers of newspaper.

VISITING THE UNITED STATES

The United States of America has now become a favourite holiday country. Food is surprisingly inexpensive, and eating out is often very good value. When shopping, the variety of choice is enormous. If you want a really lazy holiday the availability of ready-cooked foods is a delight. Facilities on caravan sites are excellent. You will undoubtedly do most of your shopping in supermarkets or in the famous American drugstores.

Currency in America is the dollar ($1), and 100 cents = 1 dollar.

COOKING IN THE UNITED STATES

If you have heard that all Americans live entirely upon convenience foods, you will soon find that this is not the case. Most Americans are good cooks and appreciate the value of first-class fresh ingredients. Their cuisine is influenced by the wide variety of countries from which their citizens originated.

The fact remains, however, that in no other place in the world will you be able to buy so many prepared mixes for every kind of cookery. These will be of great value to the holiday-maker who is anxious to spend as little time in the kitchen as possible.

Fruit and Vegetables
The range of fresh fruit and vegetables is exceptional, although it will vary according to which part of the vast country you visit.

It is interesting to be able to buy freely vegetables often

considered exotic at home, such as lima and yellow wax beans, okra (lady fingers) and sweet potatoes (yams). All of these can be cooked by our usual method, in boiling salted water, but why not be more adventurous and use some of the typical recipes of the US. Here are some ideas to try . . .

Lima beans are available in cans, and make an excellent dish when blended with chopped green peppers, grated cheese and melted butter, and then baked until the cheese melts. The more familiar haricot beans (known as navy beans in North America) can be used in the same way.

Okra is a vegetable which is sometimes called lady fingers because of the shape of the long, green fleshy pod. It makes a good partner to aubergines, which the Americans call eggplant.

Here is a stew which combines three favourite vegetables. Dice 2 medium aubergines, 6–8 okra pods, 2 red peppers (the sweet ones), with the seeds removed, and 2 medium onions. Just allow the vegetables to cook gently in a little butter for about 40 minutes, or until tender. Add salt and pepper. *Serves 4.*

Read page 73 if you want to avoid the slightly bitter taste of the aubergine.

Cooking Sweet Potatoes

This is a method of cooking sweet potatoes or yams which reflects the American liking for unexpected blendings of flavours. Wash the potato skins very well, prick, then bake in their jackets until tender. The timing for baking sweet potatoes is difficult since they vary so much in thickness as well as weight, but allow an average of 1 hour in a moderate oven, 190°C, 375°F, Gas Mark 5. Split the potatoes, scoop out the pulp, mash with butter, add a little salt, pepper and sugar, and 1–2 tablespoons seedless raisins for each portion. Spoon back into the potato skins and put back in the oven for a short while to heat through. Sweet potatoes are particularly good with poultry or ham. You can roast or mash them, but be careful that, with their high sugar content, they do not burn when roasting.

Salads

American cooks blend fruits with vegetables in salads, which is a fresh idea for holiday cooking. Serve salads as separate courses or as accompaniments to main dishes.

The best known of all American 'fruity' salads is **Waldorf**, a blending of diced celery, apples, bananas and nuts in mayonnaise.

Coleslaw is now familiar to most people. Sometimes the shredded white cabbage or tender cabbage heart is blended with orange segments and/or diced dessert apples. The cabbage can be combined with diced celery, grated raw carrot, chopped nuts and dried fruit, or with more savoury ingredients such as cucumber or gherkins, cut into match-stick shapes, and capers.

If the family have plenty of fruit and salads there is no need to worry about cooking vegetables.

Salad dressings in the United States are as varied as the salads. If you are tired of mayonnaise-based sauces use natural yoghourt (yogurt in America) or soured cream as the dressing. Add mustard (American mustard is very mild), sugar, salt and pepper to taste. This is particularly good with a coleslaw.

Fish

If you are fortunate enough to be near the coast, you will be able to find first class shell, as well as other fish. Use them to make a typical chowder, which is a thick soup, almost as satisfying as a stew. You can use all kinds of shellfish – crabs, crayfish or clams. Clams really need mincing, so if you want a clam chowder and do not have a mincer, look for canned minced clams in the supermarket. I am giving my favourite recipe for this soup, which I use with all shellfish.

Clam Chowder

Dice 2–3 rashers of fairly fat bacon and peel and finely chop or grate a medium onion. Peel and dice 2 medium potatoes and keep them in water until required. Heat the bacon and onion together in a saucepan until the bacon starts to crisp and the onion becomes pale golden. Add 300ml (½ pint-US 1¼ cups) water, and 600ml (1 pint-US 2½ cups) milk. Add the diced potatoes, a little salt and pepper, and simmer for 10 minutes. Stir about 350g (12oz-US ¾lb) minced clams, crabmeat, or other shellfish, 150ml (¼ pint-US ⅔ cup) double (heavy) cream, plus 2 or 3 plain biscuits (crackers) into the soup. Simmer for another 10 minutes, stir in a small knob of butter and serve. *Serves 4–6.*

Meat and Poultry

North America has first-class meat of all kinds, and they savour the quality in simple roast and grilled (broiled) dishes. You will be able to enjoy authentic hamburgers too! Although there are many recipes for these, Americans advocate the simplest method of all – just blend first-class minced (ground) beef with a very little salt and pepper and form into the familiar round cakes. The meat should be as freshly minced as possible.

If the meat has a good blending of lean and fat, you simply preheat the frying pan without additional fat. Put in the meat cakes and fry quickly on each side. If the meat is very lean you will need to add a small amount of fat (ask for shortening) to the pan.

Ready-cooked chickens and turkey meat abound. If you buy frozen poultry do be careful to defrost it thoroughly before roasting.

Desserts

You will be presented with an enormous range of ice cream in flavours you had never even thought of. Then there are pecan pies, pumpkin pies, lemon meringue pies and cheese cakes topped with blueberries, fresh strawberries, whipped cream sprinkled with praline.... In fact, the local ice cream parlour or delicatessen can be relied on to provide all the desserts you can eat.

Of course, the simple desserts in this book are also easily prepared with American ingredients.

American Measures

It is doubtful whether you will find domestic kitchen scales in your American holiday home. It is usual in America to buy foods by the pound, and then measure at home in cups, tablespoons and teaspoons. Ounces is a measure not used in American cookery.

Americans use the pint as a liquid measure, but it is a 16 oz pint (2 American cups), and not the 20 oz Imperial or British pint.

Here are some examples of British liquid measures in terms of American cups:

1 pint = 2½ American cups	½ pint = 1¼ American cups
¾ pint = scant 2 American cups	¼ pint = ⅔ American cup

When measuring food by the cupful or tablespoon, you have appreciable differences, as the following examples show. I have given the most common foods, and those where you need a fairly accurate measure in cooking. This will allow you to follow any recipes in this book using cup or tablespoon measures. To cut down confusion when shopping, the American name for the food is included, when it differs from the British.

The spoon measures given are American, and smaller than our tablespoon.

*1oz flour = ¼ cup or 4 tablespoons   4oz flour = 1 cup

1oz cornflour (cornstarch in US) = ¼ cup or 4 tablespoons   4½oz cornflour = 1 cup

1oz caster sugar (granulated) = 2 tablespoons   4oz sugar = ½ cup firmly packed

1oz fat (shortening) butter or margarine = 2 tablespoons   4oz fat = ½ cup butter or margarine

1oz grated Cheddar cheese = ¼ cup   4oz grated Cheddar cheese = 1 cup

4oz grated Parmesan cheese = ½ cup

1oz rice = 2 tablespoons   4oz rice = generous ½ cup

1oz golden (light corn) syrup or treacle (molasses) = 1½ tablespoons   4oz syrup = generous ⅓ cup

1oz dried fruit = 3 tablespoons   4oz dried fruit = approx ⅔ cup

*Self-raising flour is not available, so you need plain (all-purpose) flour plus baking powder.

Digestive biscuits are Graham crackers.

Double cream is heavy cream and single cream, light or coffee cream.

Biscuits are known as cookies.

Icing sugar is confectioner's sugar.

Haricot beans are navy beans.

Barbecues

You may well find barbecue equipment provided. Take advantage of this, as it is ideal holiday cooking and great fun. If your fuel is charcoal, remember to wait until it glows red before you cook. Always pre-heat the gas or electric barbecue well before cooking.

The choice of food and the timing is much the same as when using an ordinary grill. Keep foods well basted with oil, melted fat or a barbecue sauce. The latter is easily bought ready-made, but here is a version that is ideal for brushing over steaks, chops, joints of young chicken (or whole chicken) and sausages.

Barbecue Sauce

Peel and chop 2 medium onions and 1–2 cloves garlic. Blend with about 150ml (¼ pint/⅔ cup) good cooking oil, 2–3 tablespoons tomato ketchup, 1 tablespoon vinegar, 1 teaspoon (or more) of Worcestershire sauce, and a tablespoon sugar. Heat the ingredients for just a minute or two, there is no need to cook the onion and garlic. Brush the food with this before it starts to cook as well as continually as it cooks. This is enough for 4–6 steaks, chops, or chicken joints.

Vegetables and Fish

Wrap jacket potatoes and any other prepared vegetables (with plenty of butter to keep them moist and a little seasoning) in foil parcels and cook them over the barbecue fire. A medium-sized potato will take about an hour to cook; alway prick it well before wrapping.

Fish can also be cooked in foil in this way. Add butter, seasoning and a squeeze of lemon or some herbs to flavour it. This is a practical way of cooking fish in the oven too. Not only does it save washing-up and cooking smells, but it retains all the flavour of the fish. Allow about 20–25 minutes for a thick cutlet of fish, whether over the barbecue or in a moderately hot oven. It is an ideal way of cooking firm-fleshed fish, like turbot, halibut and salmon. I like to wrap each portion separately. It can then be simply tipped from the foil on to the serving plate, complete with its buttery sauce.

VISITING AUSTRIA

Austrian food is original and sophisticated. While there is a similarity to German food in some places, it tends to be lighter and to have a more subtle blending of flavours.

Although Austria is an inland country, there is a good selection of fresh-water fish from which to choose. Meat is of excellent quality with veal, pork, smoked and cured meats being the most plentiful and popular. Desserts and tortes – the Austrian gateaux – are varied and delicious. Supermarkets are much more common than small, specialist shops.

Currency in Austria is the *schilling* of 100 *groschen*.

Food shops are

Supermarket	—	*Lebensmittelgeschäft*
Butcher	—	*Fleischhauer*
Fruiterer and greengrocer	—	*Gemüse und Obsthandel*

COOKING IN AUSTRIA

Most of the recipes which follow would be warming and satisfying in colder weather, if you are visiting the country for winter sports. But they are easily adaptable for warmer days. (In summer, you would probably choose schnitzel and salad rather than a steaming bowl of goulash.)

Desserts of all kinds are easily available. Choose from the elaborate gateaux or simpler, yet equally delicious, strudels.

Soups

The recipes on page 112 are warming and satisfying, but the following are typically Austrian in flavour.

Bread Soup

Bread soup may sound odd and uninspiring, but it is in fact easy and very satisfying. It is ideal if you have some cooked Austrian sausages left from a meal. Frankfurters are only one of the many delicious varieties of sausage you can buy to serve hot.

Put 900ml (1½ pints) chicken stock into a saucepan. Austrian cooks use veal stock, but you will probably not have this and can use water with 2 chicken stock cubes. Cut or break 4 slices of rye bread into the boiling liquid and simmer for a few minutes: the bread will disintegrate and give substance to the soup. Thinly slice 4 Frankfurter or similar sausages into the soup. Stir briskly to blend the bread into the liquid. Beat 2 or 3 eggs with a little salt and pepper, whisk into the hot, but not boiling, soup and simmer gently for several minutes.

A soup with more flavour can be made by peeling and slicing 2 medium onions and frying in 25–50g (1–2oz) hot butter, before adding the liquid. *Serves 4–6.*

Gulaschsuppo

This Austrian version of goulash soup makes an excellent light meal. Peel and finely dice 2 onions and about 225g (8oz) potatoes. Keep these in cold water. Dice about 350g (12oz) lean beef (or use minced beef).

Heat 50g (2oz) fat in a saucepan, toss the onions in this, add the meat and cook for 2–3 minutes. Stir in 1 teaspoon paprika, 2 tablespoons flour (or 1 tablespoon cornflour) and stir over a low heat. Do this carefully as paprika can burn easily. Gradually blend in a generous litre (nearly 2 pints) beef stock, or water with stock cubes. Add a little salt and pepper. Bring the liquid to boiling point, lower the heat, cover the pan, and simmer for 1¼ hours. Add the diced potatoes, 1 teaspoon caraway seeds, and a little salt and pepper, if necessary. Simmer for a further 30 minutes, then serve topped with soured cream or yoghourt. *Serves 4–6.*

Tomato and Celeriac Soup

Use either a 450g (1lb) can of tomatoes, or the same weight in fresh tomatoes plus an extra 150ml (¼ pint) water. If using fresh tomatoes, peel and cut into quarters. Peel and finely dice half a celeriac root – use the other half for an hors d'oeuvre (see page 67). Put the tomatoes with their juice, or extra water, and celeriac into a saucepan with a generous 1 litre (nearly 2 pints) water, and 2 chicken stock cubes.

Bring up to boiling point, cover the pan and simmer for 10

minutes, then add 2–3 tablespoons rice, 1 tablespoon tomato purée and season to taste. Simmer steadily for 15–20 minutes, or until the rice is tender. Add chopped parsley, if you have it. *Serves 4–6.*
To vary: Chopped onions or garlic can be added for extra flavour. Add these with the tomatoes and celeriac at the beginning of the cooking period.

Meat Dishes

One always associates *Wiener Schnitzel* with Austrian cooking and although you will be able to buy good veal, you will find more plentiful supplies of pork and beef. Lamb is less popular, but you should be able to buy very young chickens, either uncooked or ready-fried.

To make the true *Wiener Schnitzel*, flatten very thin slices of veal (cut from the fillet) with a rolling pin or anything fairly solid. Coat in a little seasoned flour, beaten egg and fine breadcrumbs.

Fry the veal until tender in butter, or better still lard. If the veal slices are very thin, they should be cooked on both sides in 5–6 minutes. Serve with lemon.

If fresh breadcrumbs cause problems, follow the simpler version of this recipe given below.

Naturschnitzel

Simply dust the thin slices of veal with a little flour, salt and pepper. If frying 4 slices of veal heat 50g (2oz) butter with 25g (1oz) lard or 1 tablespoon oil. Fry the veal until tender, lift out of the pan, and add a little stock to any fat left, stir well to absorb this and pour over the meat.

This can be made more lavish by adding a little cream, lemon juice, and a few capers to the pan at the end and heating gently to make a sauce. Spoon over the meat.

Baked Frankfurters with Eggs

The wide range of sausages, often available ready-cooked, can provide interesting meals with the minimum of cooking. Frankfurters are used in the following recipe, but other similar sausages could be substituted.

Allow 1–2 Frankfurters (depending on appetite) plus 15g (½oz) butter and an egg per person. Slice the Frankfurters thinly, and put in a long dish. Melt the butter and pour over the sausages. Break the eggs carefully on top, add a very little salt and pepper and bake for about 6 minutes towards the top of a hot oven, 220°C, 425°F, Gas Mark 7.

Goulash

The Austrians have an incredible range of stews, of which their version of goulash made with pork, is famous.

Dice 0·75Kg (1½lb) shoulder pork. Peel and dice 2–3 medium onions and a thick rasher of bacon. Heat 25g (1oz) lard or other fat in a large saucepan and fry the bacon with the onions. Add ½–1 tablespoon paprika (see the note below) and stir thoroughly to prevent burning. Add the pork, 2 skinned chopped tomatoes, 300ml (½ pint) water, ½–1 teaspoon caraway seeds, and salt and pepper to taste. Cover the pan and simmer gently for about 1¼–1½ hours. Check the pan from time to time to make sure there is enough liquid.

When the pork is tender, stir in 150ml (¼ pint) soured cream, which is easily available, heat for a short time only, and serve. *Serves 4–5.*

To vary:

a) Add about 350g (12oz) sauerkraut about 45 minutes before the end of the cooking time.

b) Use diced stewing beef instead of pork, or half pork and half beef. You will need to increase the fat to at least 50g (2oz) to compensate for the leaner meat and to cook for a rather longer period. Veal can also be used, either by itself or mixed with pork and/or beef.

c) 1–2 peeled and chopped garlic cloves can be added.

d) Increase the amount of tomatoes to 450g (1lb) and the water to 450ml (¾ pint). About 35 minutes before the end of the cooking time add 450g (1lb) small peeled potatoes. This Hungarian version is ideal for holidays, as it makes a complete meal in one pan.

Note: You will be offered an amazing range of paprika in Austria, including hot paprika, which we do not often use. For a familiar flavour, select sweet paprika.

Vegetables

Naturally the severe weather in Austria during the winter months restricts the variety of vegetables available. But root vegetables, cabbage, frozen and canned vegetables provide plenty of scope for imaginative cooking.

Cook red as well as white and green cabbage. For a change, cook the shredded vegetable in a little white wine instead of water. The cabbage can be blended with fried chopped onion and flavoured with 1–2 teaspoons vinegar and the same amount of sugar, to give an interesting blending of flavour.

Try and gauge the amount of wine, so that it has all been absorbed when the cabbage is cooked.

I am sure you will not want the bother of making sauces for cauliflower, so I suggest you are gloriously extravagant and pour a little single or coffee cream over the cooked vegetable instead, and heat for a few minutes in the oven. Or use soured cream.

Sliced carrots are more interesting if you add several peeled, chopped or sliced onions as the vegetable cooks.

Salads

Austrian salads are interesting in their combination of flavours. In winter they are based upon celeriac, lightly cooked cauliflower and cabbage, as well as potatoes and tomatoes.

An Austrian cabbage salad is quite different from a coleslaw, but just as good. Shred white or red cabbage very finely and put into a bowl. Cover with boiling water, then leave until the water has cooled. Squeeze or press out the surplus moisture. Toss in an oil and vinegar dressing (see page 70) and add a few caraway seeds.

Desserts

The following two practical family desserts will probably seem even more appetizing after a day spent in the crisp, Austrian air. The wine pudding needs a fairly brisk whisking, but it does justify this effort!

Austrian Bread Pudding

This consists of an apple and dried fruit layer sandwiched between a light bread and custard mixture.

Slice 4 rolls in half, put in a basin. Whisk 2 eggs with 1 tablespoon sugar and add 300ml (½ pint) cold milk. Pour this custard over the rolls and leave for 10–15 minutes. Spoon about half this mixture into a fairly deep buttered oven-proof dish.

Peel and thinly slice about 450g (1lb) cooking apples, place over the roll and custard layer, then top with 2–3 tablespoons dried fruit, 2 tablespoons sugar and 2 tablespoons chopped blanched almonds. Spoon the rest of the roll and custard over the apple mixture, covering it completely. Bake in the centre or the coolest part of a slow oven, 150°C, 300°F, Gas Mark 2. It takes approximately 45 minutes for the custard to set and the apples to soften, but this does depend upon the depth of the mixture, and the position in the oven. *Serves 4–6.*

Wine Pudding

This consists. of a light soufflé-type pudding, flavoured with lemon and ground almonds, and served with a wine sauce. The sauce is equally good with any light sponge pudding.

You need a really deep oven-proof dish.

Spread the inside with a little butter, then sprinkle 1–2 tablespoons ground almonds over the butter. Separate the yolks from the whites of 4 eggs. Whisk the egg yolks with 1 tablespoon sugar until light and creamy, and fold in just 2 tablespoons fine dry biscuit crumbs and 4 tablespoons ground almonds, or other ground nuts.

Ground *unblanched* almonds (readily available) give more flavour. Next add the grated rind of 1 lemon.

Whisk the 4 eggs whites until stiff, fold in 2 tablespoons sugar and gently blend with the egg yolk mixture. Spoon into the dish and bake for approximately 20 minutes in the centre of a moderately hot oven, 200°C, 400°F, Gas Mark 6.

While the pudding is cooking, make the sauce. Put 2–3 tablespoons sugar into a saucepan and leave over a low heat, stirring once or twice, until a pale golden caramel. Add 150ml (¼ pint) water, 150ml (¼ pint) white wine, the grated rind of a lemon, 1 tablespoon lemon juice, and boil for several minutes. A clove and a drop or two of vanilla essence can be added for extra flavour (many recipes do). This sauce is not thickened.

Serve the pudding with the wine sauce. *Serves 4–6.*

VISITING BELGIUM

Self-catering in Belgium is very popular today, with a wide choice of villas and flats, as well as the popular camping sites.

In the delicatessen shops, or counters in supermarkets, grocers or butchers, you will find an excellent range of pâtés, cooked meats and salad dishes, rather similar to those in France. The influence of both French and Flemish cooking is obvious.

Currency in Belgium is the franc (BF).

Food shops may be indicated in either French or Flemish. There are very good supermarkets and special shops where fried potatoes are sold.

Food shops are:

		French	Dutch (Flemish)
Baker	—	*Boulangerie*	*Bakkerij*
Butcher	—	*Boucherie*	*Slagerij*
Chip stall	—	*Frites*	*Frituur*
Delicatessen	—	*Charcuterie*	*Spekslagerij*
Fishmonger	—	*Poissonnerie*	*Vishandel*
Grocer	—	*Épicerie*	*Kruidenierswinkel*
Street market	—	*Marché*	*Markt*
Supermarket	—	*Supermarché*	*Supermarkt*

COOKING IN BELGIUM

An interesting aspect of eating, shopping and cooking in Belgium is the unique blending of two entirely different cuisines, as well as languages.

French and Flemish influences combine to give a great variety of foods from which to choose. In Belgium, a selection of meats are often cooked together for a hotchpot. A simplified version of this is given on page 53.

The recipe for chicken soup, on the same page, is really a very substantial stew. The chickens in Belgium are of such good quality that they are ideal for a simple recipe, without many extra flavourings.

An unusual recipe combining rabbit with prunes is given on page 53.

Hors d'oeuvre and Fish

One of the most famous pâtés in the world, Brussels pâté, is really a terrine. It is made up of the breast of chicken layered with minced chicken meat, mixed with bacon, pork, spices and brandy.

Smoked eel is another favourite starter that you will be able to buy from supermarkets and fish shops. The fish should look pleasantly moist.

Fresh eels are one of the most popular fish in Belgium. They are tiresome and time-consuming to skin and this is not the kind of job for someone on holiday. If, however, you can buy the fish ready-skinned and cut into convenient pieces do try the dish 'green eel'. Heat a little butter in a pan and cook the fish steadily for about 10 minutes, turning several times. Add lots of chopped fresh herbs (hence the name of the dish). These can include parsley, chives, sage, chervil (a typical herb of Belgium or France, that looks like delicate parsley), savory and tarragon. Pour on wine, or wine and water, to cover. Simmer gently in a covered pan for about 15 minutes, until the fish is soft. For each 300ml (½ pint) liquid allow 2 egg yolks, 1 tablespoon lemon juice, salt and pepper to taste. Whisk into the hot liquid. Serve hot or cold as a main dish or hors d'oeuvre.

Meat and Poultry

The following recipes are ideal for satsifying meals.

Carbonnade of Beef

This has become one of the most famous stews in the world. You must try this with the excellent Belgian beer. Dice about 675g (1½lb) stewing beef and coat in 25g (1oz) seasoned flour. Peel and thinly slice 3–4 good-sized onions and dice several rashers of bacon. Heat 50g (2oz) fat and fry the onions, bacon and meat for 10 minutes, stirring continuously. Add 300ml (½ pint) beer (choose light ale for a delicate taste, dark beer for a rich flavour) and the same amount of beef stock or water with a stock cube. Stir well and bring to the boil. Add a little salt, pepper and sugar to taste. Some recipes add a tablespoon of vinegar. Cover; simmer for about 2 hours. This can also be cooked in a covered casserole in the oven, set at a low heat. *Serves 4–6.*

Rabbit with Prunes

Ideally dried prunes should be used for this dish. But canned, drained prunes can be added when the rabbit is nearly cooked.

Ask for a young rabbit, and have it jointed. Soak overnight in 450ml (¾ pint) red wine, 2 tablespoons red wine vinegar and 2 bay leaves.

Soak about 175g (6oz) prunes in cold water, or put them to soak with the rabbit. Lift the rabbit from the liquid, drain well and coat in 25g (1oz) seasoned flour. Fry until golden in 50g (2oz) butter and stir in the wine and vinegar. Bring the liquid to the boil and stir until slightly thickened. Add the well-drained prunes, 1–2 tablespoons redcurrant jelly (or red jam, such as plum), and season to taste. Cover the pan and simmer gently for 1½ hours. *Serves 4.*

Chicken Soup

Simmer a good-sized chicken with diced vegetables, chopped herbs and seasoning to taste in water and white wine until tender. Serve the sliced chicken, vegetables and some of the stock topped with soft breadcrumbs and chopped parsley.

Le Hotchpot

Put small joints of beef, lamb or mutton, and veal into a large saucepan. Add pig's feet and ears (if desired) with diced vegetables, chopped herbs, water to cover and seasoning. Simmer until the meat is tender. Serve hot or cold. Belgian sausages can be added towards the end of the cooking time. Obviously, this is a recipe which is infinitely adaptable, according to the ingredients at hand.

Vegetables

These are similar to those found in most countries of Northern Europe. Belgium however does specialize in the vegetable which we call chicory, the French call *endive* and the Belgians call *witloof*. Its white head is delicious eaten raw, but equally good when cooked.

Wash the heads, pack into a greased ovenproof dish and add

just 2–3 tablespoons water, 25–50g (1–2oz) butter or margarine plus a little salt and pepper. Cover the dish with greased foil or a lid and bake in the centre of a very moderate oven, 160°C, 325°F, Gas Mark 3 for about 30 minutes, or until the chicory is just soft; do not overcook it, it should keep its shape.

Chicory in Brown Butter

Heat 50–75g (2–3oz) butter in a frying pan and cook 4 heads of chicory until just tender. Lift the vegetable on to a hot dish or individual plates. Allow the butter to turn golden brown, add a squeeze of lemon juice, salt and pepper to taste, then pour over the vegetables.

Asparagus

If you are fortunate enough to be in Belgium when asparagus is in season serve this in the national style. Soft-boil an egg for each person. Shell the hot eggs, mash with 25g (1oz) butter to each egg, salt and pepper, then add a little chopped parsley. Spoon this sauce-like mixture over the asparagus.

Hop Shoots

Since Belgium produces good beer, you may be able to buy hop shoots, which can be cooked as an unusual and delicious vegetable. Wash the hops and put them into a little boiling water, flavoured with lemon juice, salt and pepper. Boil until tender (between 10–15 minutes), drain and top with melted butter or with cream. Hops and poached eggs are a good combination and a pleasant change from spinach and eggs.

Red Cabbage

Shred red cabbage very finely, toss in about 50g (2oz) butter or margarine, then cook in a very little water with salt, pepper, a teaspoon of sugar and 2 teaspoons vinegar. Cover the saucepan and simmer gently until the cabbage is tender and the surplus liquid has evaporated. The cabbage can also be cooked in the top of a double saucepan, over boiling water.

VISITING DENMARK

Shopping in Denmark, like other Scandinavian countries, is relatively easy due to the high proportion of people who speak and understand a certain amount of English.

There are excellent supermarkets and self-service shops. Dairy produce is particularly good, and you can buy really sustaining sandwiches from special shops.

Currency in Denmark is the *krone* (DKr) of 100 *øre*.

Food shops are

Baker	—	*Bager*
Butcher	—	*Slagter*
Dairy	—	*Mejeri*
Fruiterer and greengrocer	—	*Grønthandler*

COOKING IN DENMARK

Although each Scandinavian country has its own distinctive dishes, they have many similar foods and methods of cooking. I have therefore grouped the Scandinavian recipes on pages 96 to 100.

If one had to select one outstanding dish that has given Denmark its reputation for good food it would be *Smørrebrød*. This word is used to describe a table of small appetisers, but is better known as the name for the fabulous Danish open sandwiches. Open sandwiches are served in all of the Scandinavian countries, but they originated in Denmark and it is in this country that you will find restaurants offering a wide selection of these colourful and satsifying meals. I use the term 'meals' because most *Smørrebrød* are sufficiently satsifying to be served for lunch.

Buy a selection of ready-prepared *Smørrebrød*, which will be beautifully packed for you to carry. The various ingredients are blended together skilfully to give a variety of colours, textures and flavours. It takes long practice to achieve this high standard of presentation, but the ready-prepared variety should stimulate your own artistic ability!

A selection of *Smørrebrød* toppings is given on page 56.

To Make *Smørrebrød*

Choose fresh white, brown, wholemeal or rye bread, cut thinly and spread generously with butter. Top with lettuce before adding the toppings.

Serve the sandwiches with a knife and fork, as they are too difficult to eat with your fingers. If packing these for a picnic, top each sandwich with a square of waxed or greaseproof paper to take the place of the top slice of bread and butter in traditional sandwiches. Of course the sandwich habit of Scandinavia is ideal for holiday meals.

Some of the most popular *Smørrebrød* toppings are:

Meat Liver pâté with well-drained pickled cabbage and sliced fresh orange or well-drained mandarin oranges or lingonberry preserve (lingonberries are wild cranberries and very popular as an accompaniment to game, meat and poultry).

Liver pâté with cooked prunes, crisp bacon rashers and Russian salad.

Sliced beef with horseradish-flavoured mayonnaise, potato and Russian salads.

Generously thick slices of chicken with rolls of ham or crisp bacon, mayonnaise, grapes and watercress.

Fish Shrimps or prawns with sliced cucumber, sliced tomato, twists of lemon and excellent mayonnaise (this is sold in tubes rather than jars).

Fried crisp fillets of fish with lemon-flavoured mayonnaise, cucumber and potato salad, topped with chopped dill. (The fish is cold.)

Smoked fish (eel, mackerel, salmon) combined with cold scrambled egg, topped with chopped dill and garnished with cucumber and lemon.

Danish caviar (cheaper than Beluga!) with hard-boiled egg, onion rings, lemon twists.

Cheese Invest in a cheese slicer, which is not expensive, and will enable you to slice cheeses expertly.

There are many interesting cheeses to use; page 90 gives some of the range of cheeses you will find in Denmark. Slice thinly, put on the bread, butter and lettuce and garnish with fruit or vegetable salads.

VISITING FINLAND

Finland boasts breathtaking scenery and a peaceful, unspoiled atmosphere. The relaxed atmosphere makes it ideal for self-catering holidays.

Currency in Finland is the *markka* (Fmk) divisible into 100 *penniä* (p).

Most camping and caravan sites have their own shops, and the supermarkets and mobile shops are very good.

Supermarket	—	*Itsepalvelumyymälä*
Mobile shop	—	*Myymäläauto*
Baker	—	*Leipomo*
Butcher	—	*Lihakauppa*
Dairy	—	*Maitokauppa*
Fruiterer and greengrocer	—	*Hedelmäkauppa*
Grocer	—	*Siirtomaatavarakauppa*

COOKING IN FINLAND

Finland is considered a Scandinavian country and the foods and recipes given on pages 96 to 100 apply to this country. There is a definite Russian influence in some dishes.

Finland has no Atlantic coastline but you will be able to buy excellent freshwater fish, caught in the lakes, tiny herrings the size of sprats from the Baltic and crayfish. At the start of the crayfish season, in July, there are special parties to celebrate the catch.

You can buy reindeer meat, which is very similar in flavour to venison. If you dislike very highly-flavoured game, soak the meat in milk before cooking. It can be used in casseroles, or thinly sliced and fried or roasted.

Vegetables are limited, due to the very severe winter climate but there are root vegetables, cabbage, cauliflower and spinach, and a good selection of different kinds of mushrooms.

Easy Fish Dishes
The following typically Finnish ways of cooking fish are ideal for holiday meals.

Fish Baked in Bread

Buy a good-sized loaf. Cut a slice from one end, set this aside, then scoop out most of the centre crumb, leaving a large hollow for stuffing. The bread removed can be used in cooking. (Soups and stews can be thickened with bread rather than flour. Bread softens and 'disappears' in the liquid and cannot become lumpy, like flour.)

Buy a good 450g (1lb) fish for 4 people, remove the heads, tails, clean and dry the fish, season it well and put into the loaf together with several rashers of de-rinded and chopped bacon. Press the end slice back in position. Stand the filled loaf on a sheet of foil, spread the loaf thickly with butter and wrap it in the foil. Bake very slowly, 150°C, 300°F, Gas Mark 2, for about 2½ hours, then leave to cool in the foil. Cut in slices to serve. This is an ideal picnic dish. *Serves 4–6.*

Fish Casserole

Use a white fish or filleted fresh herrings for this dish. (Remove the heads, tails and bones.) Cut the white fish into neat pieces and each fillet of herring into 2 or 3 portions. To 450g (1lb) prepared fish use 450g (1lb) peeled and thinly sliced potatoes, 2 peeled and thinly sliced onions and 2 rashers of de-rinded and chopped bacon. Arrange the food in layers in a greased casserole, finishing with potatoes. Beat 2 eggs with 450ml (¾ pint) milk, adding salt, pepper and a good pinch powdered bay leaf.

Pour this over the fish mixture, then top with 25–50g (1–2oz) butter and bake for about 1 hour in the centre of a very moderate oven, 160°C, 325°F, Gas Mark 3. Serve hot with baked mushrooms and spinach. *Serves 4–6.*

VISITING FRANCE

France provides a unique range of food for the family who are catering for themselves. If you feel lazy, simply visit the *charcuterie* counter or stall at the local market, where you will find an amazing selection of pâtés, cooked meats and other dishes. The fish, fruit and vegetables are excellent, and of course French bread, always freshly baked, is delicious.

Croissants are a holiday treat. Try also *pains au chocolat* – small rolls like croissants, filled with plain chocolate which are heated in the oven before eating.

French wines need no introduction. Local wines are usually inexpensive and good.

The currency in France is the *franc*, and there are 100 *centimes* to one franc.

Supermarkets (*Supermarchés*) are now very popular in France. There are, however, still many family shops which give excellent service. Milk is sold in supermarkets and grocers, not in special dairies.

Food shops are:

Baker	—	*Boulangerie*
Butcher	—	*Boucherie*
Fishmonger	—	*Poissonerie*
Grocer	—	*Epicerie*
Fruiterer and greengrocer	—	*Legumes, Fruitier*

COOKING IN FRANCE

One of the best ways to learn of the specialities of France is to look at menus displayed outside cafés and restaurants, and see what the *plat de jour* or set menu offers. This is a fair indication of the kind of food that is particularly good in that neighbourhood.

Hors d'oeuvre and Fish

One of the easiest hors d'oeuvre in France is pâté, for this is not only excellent but incredibly varied. Each region has its own speciality. Some of these are so satisfying that they can, with salad, provide a light meal.

Fresh melons are plentiful and cheap, and in many areas you can obtain good fresh figs. Melon or figs served with smoked ham make a luxurious light main dish or hors d'oeuvre.

Coastal areas provide an exciting array of shell, as well as fresh white fish. Lobsters are even more expensive than in Britain, but some of the other shell fish, such as oysters, are remarkably inexpensive if they are a speciality of the area. If oysters are cheap, they can be coated with seasoned flour or cornflour, and fried as a change from eating them raw.

Other shell fish, prawns and shrimps, scallops and a clam-type *palourde* can be used in the chowder on page 41 or eaten like an oyster, without cooking.

All the fish recipes in this book can be adapted to the great variety of white fish you are likely to find in France. The excellent French sole should not be cooked when it is freshly caught, if it is kept in a cool place for at least 12 hours, and preferably 24 hours, it reaches full maturity of flavour and tenderness.

Many fish are of similar varieties to ours, but you will find others we do not know. There is a preponderence of red and grey mullet, and the popular fish in the south of France is the sea-perch or sea bass.

Of course you cannot visit France without enjoying mussels, and several recipes using these, as well as other shell and various types of fish, are to be found on pages 41, 82, 94 and 111.

Simple fish dishes need good flavourings and one can always buy fresh herbs. Keep a good-sized bunch in your kitchen or your tent. They make a gay bouquet and give an enticing smell.

Bouquet Garni

Generally consists of a sprig of parsley, thyme and a bay leaf tied together. Other herbs you will find used in France are basil, chervil, chives, rosemary, sage and tarragon.

Meat, Poultry and Game

Meat is expensive in France, and the quality can be variable. But you can get excellent beef and lamb and very good pork and veal. The French method of cutting meat ensures that almost all the meat is edible. I have included recipes using all these meats on pages 62 to 65.

If you feel you must have your traditional roast joint, you will be unpleasantly surprised at the price. I would suggest you concentrate upon small cuts of meat, augmented by some of the plentiful, delicious vegetables.

If you are fond of offal, like brains, kidneys and liver, these are excellent in quality. Frozen food manufacturers freeze foods that are appreciated in that particular country, so you can obtain frozen brains, which just need cooking in butter and serving with lemon. The fresh brains should be soaked in plenty of salted cold water for an hour, drained, rinsed, then cooked. Black and white puddings can be found among the prepared meats. I like them sliced and fried gently, then served with crisp rings of fried cooking or dessert apple.

Chickens

You may well find two entirely different looking chickens in shops: one rather yellow in colour, the other pristine white and very plump. May I advise choosing the yellowish bird. It is this colour because it has been corn-fed, and has a real old-fashioned flavour. There are many recipes in this book using chicken, many of them based upon ready-cooked chickens, which are popular in most countries. If your family like stuffings with roast chicken, then look out for canned chestnut purée, which is much cheaper than at home. Add a little salt and pepper to the *unsweetened* purée, plus a good knob of butter or margarine, or a little chopped ham or bacon, and heat gently for a luxury stuffing with the minimum of trouble.

Guinea-fowl

This has a pleasant, gamey flavour and can be used in place of chicken. It is a very dry-fleshed bird and must therefore be kept well-moistened during cooking. You may find pigeons, pheasants and quail available, and the recipe on page 119 can be adapted for these.

Rabbit

This is a favourite food, and good quality rabbits are common. Young rabbits can be used in place of chicken in recipes where indicated.

Dishes with Beef

The French have many classic and simple dishes using beef, some made with prime meat, others with cheaper cuts. Ideas suitable for holiday catering are given on this and the following pages.

Steak Dishes

The most popular steaks are fillet, used generally for the very tender rounds (tournedos) and the cut of beef the French call *contrefilet*. This is a confusing term for it sounds like the fillet, but it is in fact a sirloin steak. Both tournedos or sirloin steak can be fried or grilled.

When frying steak add chopped tarragon, thyme or parsley and a little red or white wine to the pan just before serving the meat and stir in all the juices; this provides an easy but appetizing sauce.

Steaks are excellent served on a bed of *ratatouille*, made as on page 118.

Boeuf à la Mode

This is a classic way of cooking a piece of topside of beef. The following recipe is a simplified version of this dish.

The classic way to introduce fat into this lean joint is to insert strips of fat pork or bacon through the joint. But as this takes time and needs a proper larding needle, I suggest you are instead very generous with the amount of butter, or butter and bacon, in which you fry the meat.

Heat a good knob of butter in a strong saucepan with a little diced fat bacon or pork. Turn the joint of meat in this until pleasantly brown on either side; add enough white wine to half-cover the meat. Simmer gently in an uncovered pan for a short time, turning the meat once or twice, until the wine has almost all evaporated; this flavours the meat.

Put in a selection of vegetables, plus a chopped calf's foot (this is optional) and a bouquet garni. Add water, plus a beef stock cube and a little white wine, to *just* cover the meat. Season to taste and simmer gently, allowing about 40–45 minutes per 450g (1lb). The liquid can be thickened if desired at the end of the cooking period (see opposite).

This joint is equally good hot or cold.

Freezing: When frozen as a whole cooked joint the beef tends to lose flavour.

Provençal-style Beef

Cut about 675g (1½lb) stewing beef into neat fingers, dice 2 or 3 rashers fat bacon, peel and quarter 3–4 onions, peel and thickly slice several carrots and chop enough parsley to give 2–3 tablespoons, also peel and chop 2 cloves of garlic.

Roll the beef in seasoned flour and the chopped parsley. Heat 2 tablespoons oil in a saucepan, then add the bacon and beef and cook for 5–6 minutes, stirring from time to time.

Add approximately 300ml (½ pint) red wine and 450ml (¾ pint) water with a beef stock cube, together with a bouquet garni, the vegetables, including the garlic, salt and pepper to taste and several strips of orange rind.

Cover the saucepan and simmer gently for about 2½ hours. To make a change, try adding 1–2 tablespoons tomato purée and a few olives before serving. Serve with pasta, rice or potatoes.

If more convenient, this can be cooked in a covered casserole in a low oven. *Serves 4–6.*

Freezing: This freezes well for up to 3 months, although the wine loses some of its flavour.

To Thicken Stews

Thickening the liquid in a stew or casserole takes time, but often gives a more pleasing and appetizing dish.

It is quite possible that your temporary store cupboard does not include flour or cornflour. In this case, add soft pieces of bread (without the crusts) to the liquid, simmer for a time, then beat until smooth. The bread is absorbed by the liquid. This is also an excellent way of using up leftover French bread, which goes stale very quickly.

Another way of thickening the liquid is to cook diced potatoes in it, allowing them to break up and form a purée. Instant dehydrated potatoes are excellent for this. Blend with a little liquid and stir into the stew or casserole. Instant potato has the advantage of never forming lumps, in fact it is very similar to the potato flour used in many continental countries.

Thickening with potatoes or potato flour also gives a better texture in freezing.

Dishes with Veal

You will find a good selection of veal in butchers' shops. On the whole, this is one of the less expensive meats in France. Grill or fry chops, using plenty of butter and/or oil to keep the lean meat moist. Cook slices of veal (escalopes) following the recipes on page 47.

A joint of veal can be cooked with vegetables, as in Boeuf à la Mode on page 62, but allow slightly longer per 450g (1lb). Stewing veal can be cooked slowly with vegetables, as in the following recipe.

Veal Fricassée

Dice 675g (1½lb) stewing veal. Heat 50g (2oz) butter in a saucepan, add the veal and fry for several minutes, but do not allow the meat to brown. Add enough chicken stock, or water plus a chicken stock cube, to cover the meat, together with several peeled, sliced carrots, 2 or 3 sliced large or about 12 whole small onions or shallots. Put in a little diced bacon, a bouquet garni, salt and pepper to taste and the juice and finely pared rind of half a lemon. Cover the pan and simmer gently for 1½ hours, or until the veal is tender.

When the meat is cooked, the next step is to make the delicious creamy sauce. If you have a second saucepan, use this method: carefully strain off most of the stock from the veal and vegetables into a bowl or jug. Measure out and reserve 300ml (½ pint) of this stock. Discard the rest (or keep it to use in soups, gravies or sauces). In your second saucepan melt 50g (2oz) butter and stir in 40g (1½oz) flour. Cook gently for 2–3 minutes and then gradually blend in 300ml (½ pint) milk and the reserved 300ml (½ pint) of the veal stock. Bring to the boil, stirring continuously, and cook until thickened. Spoon the veal and vegetables into the sauce, simmer for a short time to heat, then add salt and pepper to taste.

If you only have one saucepan, pour away most of the stock, leaving only about 300ml (½ pint). Blend the flour with the milk (quantities above) and add to the liquid, together with the 50g (2oz) butter. Bring slowly to the boil, stirring continuously, and cook until thickened. For a more luxurious dish, blend in a little cream before serving. *Serves 4–6.*

Dishes with Pork

Grill, fry or bake the very excellent French pork cutlets or chops.
Fry apple rings with the pork (these take the place of apple sauce).

Joints of pork are roasted in the usual way. Add cored, but not
peeled, whole dessert apples and peeled onions to the meat tin for
appetizing accompaniments. Turn the apples and onions round in
the pork fat so they keep moist during cooking. Sprinkle with a
little brown sugar towards the end of the cooking period to glaze.

Dishes with Lamb

Lamb cutlets, chops or joints are expensive in France, but the
meat is usually excellent in quality. Fry or grill chops or cutlets
and roast a joint. Insert a few very thin slices of peeled garlic or
rosemary sprigs under the skin of the meat before roasting for an
interesting flavour with the minimum of trouble.

Navarin of Lamb

This dish is similar to boiled lamb, but the French add a generous
selection of young vegetables, such as baby turnips and carrots,
new potatoes and onions, to the meat and stock, together with a
large bunch of parsley or chervil, a little garlic (optional) and
rosemary. You can cook inexpensive middle neck chops or part of
a leg of lamb (or mutton) in this way. Allow about 1½ hours
gentle simmering if using chops and 40–45 minutes per 450g
(1lb) if cooking a whole joint. A little tomato purée can be added
to give more colour to the unthickened liquid. If any cooked lamb
is left add this to a creamy sauce made with the cooking liquid,
butter, flour, and milk, as in the recipe for Veal Fricassée on page
64.

Making Stock

In most meat dishes a good stock is necessary. Obviously you will
not have time to cook bones to make this, but you can use beef or
chicken stock cubes with water. Always be wary when adding salt
to a recipe if using a stock cube, for they are usually fairly salty.

Vegetables

These are superb, whether you buy them in shops or in the
market. Inspect them, as would a French shopper, very critically,

and pick out the particular produce you think best. The shop-keeper will respect your judgment if you do. Serve vegetables by themselves as an hors d'oeuvre, or as a separate course, in true French fashion. Some of the vegetables considered luxurious in Britain are commonplace in this warmer climate, especially in the south. Here are those I would buy and use:

Artichokes

Although Jerusalem artichokes are popular in France, they are less likely to be available in summer. If you can get them, scrub them well, do not peel, and boil in salted water. They are also delicious if scraped or peeled and grated, then served raw in salads. But the artichoke that is a speciality of France, like Italy, is the globe artichoke – the big green bud-like vegetable. Simply cut away the base of the stem and any tough-looking outer leaves. Cook steadily in plenty of boiling salted water in a saucepan (if you are short of saucepans use a roasting tin, covered with foil, in a moderately hot oven). The cooking time varies enormously with the size of the artichoke, but allow 25 minutes for smallish ones and up to 35–40 minutes for the giants. To tell if they are cooked, test if the outer leaves can be pulled off easily, and if the pulp at the base of the leaf is quite tender.

To eat the artichoke, either serve with melted butter, or with an oil and vinegar dressing (vinaigrette) – see page 70. You pull off the leaves and dip the base in the hot butter or the dressing, and eat just this tender end. When you get to the heart of the artichoke you will find the hairy 'choke', which you cannot eat, and which under most sophisticated circumstances is often removed while hot, and the centre filled with fish mixtures, butter or dressing. I feel this is too much of a refinement for holidays! At the bottom of the choke though, is the artichoke bottom, often called 'heart', which is eaten with a knife and fork. If all this sounds a great deal of trouble, excellent canned artichoke hearts are available.

Beans

Green beans are good and there are plenty of frozen narrow *haricots verts* as well as canned beans. If your children feel life is incomplete without baked beans, you will find plenty of cans in supermarkets.

Celeriac

Perhaps one of the favourite root vegetables in France. The real name is celery-root (*celeri-rave*), and it looks like an ugly mis-shapen turnip. It discolours quickly, so it must be cooked or put into a dressing as soon as peeled. The favourite way of serving is in a *remoulade* dressing as an hors d'oeuvre. Blend mustard with mayonnaise. While the exact amounts vary according to personal taste, 1 tablespoon Dijon or other French mustard to each 150ml (¼ pint) mayonnaise is usual. Add a squeeze of lemon juice too if you wish, then peel and coarsely grate the raw celeriac into the dressing. Serve topped with chopped parsley; it is excellent.

Courgettes

These baby marrows are excellent throughout the year. They are very easy to prepare: simply wash, and trim the tough ends. Dry and slice or dice. Cook in the very minimum of boiling salted water, or with chopped or sliced fresh tomatoes (to provide the necessary liquid) for about 15 minutes; do not over-cook. You will find recipes using courgettes on pages 85 and 118.

There is a wide selection of other vegetables, all beautifully fresh. You will find the large tomatoes, typical of Mediterranean areas – ridged and bumpy but excellent in salads. Choose plum-shaped tomatoes for cooking. The baby leeks that abound in France can be washed, sliced thinly and added to salads; or boil them whole until just tender, drain and wrap a rasher of bacon round each leek, grill or bake until the bacon is crisp.

If you are in France during the asparagus season you may be able to buy this at a reasonable price. If you have no deep saucepans, lay the asparagus in your roasting tin, just covered with lightly salted water. Cover tightly with foil, and cook in a moderately hot oven until tender.

The variety of vegetables available in Southern France will encourage you to make the classic vegetable stew, *ratatouille*, recipe on page 118.

Desserts

I have given some simple desserts on pages 49, 50 and 123 in case your family feel their meals are incomplete without them. But fruit and cheese are so outstandingly good in France I think you will enjoy having these instead. You can also buy excellent, if expensive, fruit tarts and pastries at the *patisserie*.

Do experiment with the range of cheeses: there are over 300 from which to choose in the whole of France, and each area will produce some interesting varieties.

The following economical French dessert is ridiculously simple, and makes good use of stale bread.

Pain-Perdu

Make sandwiches of thin slices of bread and butter and jam or marmalade. Beat an egg with a little milk and sugar and soak the sandwiches in this for a short time, but do not allow the bread to become too soggy, or it will break. Heat a little butter or margarine in a frying pan and fry the bread on each side until crisp and golden. Serve at once, sprinkled with a little sugar. This dish is good enough for a dinner party at home – it tastes like a very special fritter! There is no need to cut away the crusts.

Oeufs à la Neige

Another very simple, but very excellent French dessert.

Put 600ml (1 pint) milk into a deep frying pan; add 1 tablespoon sugar and a little vanilla essence if you have it, or one or two strips of lemon rind if you have no vanilla. Separate the yolks from the whites of 3 eggs. Whisk the egg whites until really stiff, then gradually fold in 75g (3oz) sugar. Bring the milk in the frying pan just to boiling point, and lower the heat so it simmers steadily. Drop spoonfuls of the meringue mixture on to the milk. Poach for about 2 minutes then turn with a spoon, or better still a fish slice, and poach on the other side for the same time. Lift the cooked meringues (they are cooked, although they look and feel soft), on to a sieve or something similar to drain. Strain the milk over the egg yolks and stir over a low heat until the custard has thickened. Allow to cool and put into a dish, then top with the meringues.

VISITING GERMANY

You will find it easy to shop for food in Germany. There are excellent food departments in every large department store (*Kaufhaus*). There are also chainstores in Germany from which one can buy a wide range of foods – look for names such as *Edeka*, *Spar*, *Co-op* and *Konsum*. The wide range of sausages and canned foods help to make self-catering easy and labour-saving. Milk is obtainable from supermarkets and grocers.

The currency in Germany is the *Deutsche Mark* (DM), and there are 100 *pfennig* (pfg) to the DM.

The shops from which you will buy food are:

Baker	—	*Bäckerei*
Butcher	—	*Metzger* or *Fleischhändler*
Fruiterer and greengrocer	—	*Obst-und Gemüsehändler*
Grocer	—	*Lebensmittel*

COOKING IN GERMANY

Germans have healthy appetites and their food is fairly sustaining. Holiday-makers will find delicatessen counters a delight. They are full of varied smoked and other sausages, pickled meats and vegetables, such as sauerkraut. To heat the sauerkraut, add a little wine or water and a good knob of butter or margarine, and simmer for about 30 minutes. Allow the small amount of liquid to evaporate.

Germany can offer a wide range of fish, including fresh, pickled and salt herrings, and fresh mackerel. These make excellent salads. The white fish is varied and plentiful, and there is an interesting selection of frozen fish too. Some of the recipes of Scandinavia are popular in Germany also.

Veal and pork are favourite meats in Germany.

Mackerel Salads
Smoked and fresh mackerel should be available in Germany; you could also use herrings.

The following recipe uses an unusual combination of flavours and can be served hot or cold.

Mackerel and Gingerbread

Peel and chop 2 medium onions, clean 4 mackerel, remove the heads and back bones and fillet if desired.

If serving cold: simmer the onions in seasoned water to cover until tender, drain well. Meanwhile cook the mackerel in a dish in the oven, or a pan, in a little white wine vinegar until tender. Crumble 175g (6oz) gingerbread into crumbs, blend with wine vinegar to make a paste, add 2 teaspoons sugar or syrup. Spread on to plates or a dish, top with the fish, then the onions and garnish with parsley and lemon.

If serving hot: cook the onions and mackerel together in 300ml (½ pint) well seasoned water, with a little wine vinegar to flavour. Stir in 3 tablespoons gingerbread crumbs to thicken the liquid, heat for 2–3 minutes then serve. *Serves 4.*

Mackerel in Sharp Sauce

Make the sauce by blending together 1 tablespoon made mustard (the continental type), 1 tablespoon sugar, 1 tablespoon lemon juice, grated rind of 1 lemon, 4 tablespoons white wine vinegar, a little salt, pepper and 2 tablespoons chopped parsley or dill or fennel leaves.

Hard-boil and chop 2–3 eggs; flake the flesh from 4 smoked or cooked mackerel. Dice 3–4 cooked potatoes and a medium-sized peeled beetroot.

Blend all of these ingredients with the sauce, then spoon on to a bed of lettuce and garnish with sliced pickled or fresh cucumber and more beetroot. *Serves 4–6.*

To vary: If you feel the dressing may be too sharp use a vinaigrette dressing made by blending 4 tablespoons olive, or good salad oil with a little made mustard and 1–2 tablespoons white wine vinegar or lemon juice. Add salt, pepper and a little sugar if you like a sweet dressing.

These basic proportions may be too oily for mackerel, in which case adjust the amount of oil accordingly.

Chopped fresh herbs, varied according to their availability and the dish, can be added but you cannot then make up larger quantities of the dressing to store.

VISITING GIBRALTAR

The advantage of shopping in Gibraltar is that sterling is the legal currency and, although there is a delightful Spanish atmosphere in many places, the language is English.

Many shops sell take-away food, ranging from British fish and chips to Spanish, Chinese and Indian foods. There are plenty of supermarkets and food shops.

Currency in Gibraltar is the pound.

COOKING IN GIBRALTAR

Although it is easy to shop in Gibraltar it is not now as easy to obtain as wide a variety of foods as it was before the frontiers to Spain were closed. Most foods obtainable are similar to those available in Britain, so will appeal to people who prefer familiar dishes.

Fruit and Vegetables

Excellent fruit and vegetables are all imported to 'The Rock' from Morocco and you can buy these, with local fish, from the shops or market.

Wine is inexpensive.

The warm climate will encourage you to plan relatively light meals and you will find a selection of recipes for suitable dishes throughout the book. The following dessert uses the local fruit and wine cleverly.

Fruit Syllabub

0·5kg (1lb) soft fruit
50–75g (2–3oz) sugar
300ml (½ pint) double cream
150ml (¼ pint) sweet white wine
1 tablespoon lemon juice

Prepare the fruit and divide into 4–6 portions. Put into individual dishes or cups, and sprinkle with half the sugar. Whip the cream until it holds its shape, add the rest of the sugar, and gradually blend in the wine and lemon juice.

Spoon over the fruit just before serving. Serve as cold as possible. *Serves 4–6.*

VISITING GREECE

During the past years Greece and the idyllic Greek islands have become increasingly popular for holidays. It is not a country where you will find many prepared foods, but it abounds in fresh ingredients.

Currency in Greece is the *drachma* (Dr) of 100 *lepta*.

Supermarkets or general stores sell a variety of foods, including some fruit and vegetables.

COOKING IN GREECE

One cannot mention cooking in Greece without emphasising the use of lemons and oil. *Avgolemono* is a word that appears on most menus and it means that the food will have a refreshing flavour based on egg and lemons. There is an Avgolemono Sauce to serve with fish, meat and poultry as well as a famous soup. The recipes are given below.

One of the famous dishes of Greece, Moussaka, has become world-famous. You may already have your own favourite recipe, but you will enjoy making this dish in its birthplace. I have adapted one of my favourite recipes for holiday-makers. It is on the opposite page.

The vegetables are similar to those of Italy and France, and there is an abundance of aubergines (or eggplants). It is so tempting to find these in such perfect condition that I have included several aubergine recipes on page 74.

Avgolemono Sauce (and Soup)

Whisk the yolks of 4 eggs, or 2–3 whole eggs, until light and fluffy; gradually whisk in 4 tablespoons lemon juice. This is the basis of the sauce, which can be varied in so many ways.

With fish: fry, bake or grill the fish and coat with the sauce.

With chicken: simmer the chicken with vegetables. Drain the chicken and vegetables. Whisk about 300ml (½ pint) of the stock into the Avgolemono Sauce. Heat gently, then pour over the chicken.

As a soup: simmer 50g (2oz) rice in about 900ml (1½ pints)

chicken stock until the rice is tender, then whisk in the sauce and serve.

Moussaka

When you visit Greece, and taste their famous Moussaka, you will realize there is not one recipe for this dish, but many. Some omit meat, others are soft in texture, others (mostly influenced by Turkey) quite firm like a cake.

I am giving a simple recipe that needs less preparation than many; obviously you can use potatoes instead of courgettes, and rather less aubergines if desired.

Buy 450g (1lb) minced raw meat: this can be of any kind, but mutton tends to have a better flavour. Peel and slice 2 onions, slice about 450g (1lb) unpeeled courgettes and 2–3 medium aubergines (see comments about preventing the skin being bitter given below). Heat several tablespoons oil and fry the vegetables until they begin to soften; season well.

Put layers of well-seasoned meat, vegetables, yoghourt and grated cheese into an ovenproof dish.

Top the last layer with plenty of yoghourt and a layer of cheese. Cover the dish and bake in the centre of a very moderate oven, 160°C, 325°F, Gas Mark 3 for just over an hour. Remove lid and brown under a grill or in hot oven for a few minutes.

I find layers of yoghourt and grated cheese make an easy alternative to a sauce, but if you wish to use a sauce, make it with 40g (1½oz) butter or margarine, 40g (1½oz) flour, 450ml (¾ pint) milk, seasoning, and about 175g (6oz) grated cheese, plus an egg if desired. *Serves 4–6.*

Using Aubergines

Aubergines can be used in simple, but very appetizing ways. The vegetable can be fried, as suggested on page 83, baked, or used in a pâté.

Some people dislike the rather bitter taste of aubergine skin. To minimize this flavour, wash, dry and score the skin with a knife. Sprinkle with salt, and leave for about 30 minutes. Rinse the aubergines and use. The salt draws out the juices from the skin, and removes the strong taste. Of course they can be peeled, but that is a pity, as the peel gives colour, as well as flavour.

Baked Aubergines

I like to halve aubergines, brush the cut surfaces with a little oil, add a sprinkling of salt and pepper, and bake for about 30 minutes in a hot oven, or longer at a cooler temperature, until the pulp is soft.

There are many ways in which this vegetable can be stuffed. I have avoided mixtures that need a lot of preparation, and suggest the following as being simple, as well as full of flavour.

Stuffed Aubergines

Wash, dry and halve 2 very large, or 4 smaller aubergines. If you dislike the slightly bitter taste of the skin, follow the directions on page 73. Put the halved vegetables into an oiled oven-proof dish; top the cut surfaces with a little oil. Cover the dish with a lid or foil and bake in a moderately hot oven, 200°C, 400°F, Gas Mark 6, for 25 minutes, or until soft enough to scoop out the centre pulp. Chop this, blend with 100g (4oz) chopped cooked ham, 100g (4oz) diced or grated cheese, a little chopped parsley or other herbs and a shake of salt and pepper. Spoon into the hollowed-out aubergine cases, and return to the oven for 15 minutes. Serve with baked tomatoes or a mixed salad. *Serves 4.*

Aubergine Pâté

Bake aubergines until soft as in previous recipe, mash pulp with salt, pepper, a little crushed garlic, lemon juice, and olive oil to taste. This is delicious as an hors d'oeuvre or spread, and appeals particularly to vegetarians.

I also like to blend the aubergine mixture with cream or cottage cheese to give a more pronounced taste and a firmer texture. It then becomes a lovely sandwich filling – ideal for packing with some Greek bread and wine for a picnic in an olive grove.

VISITING HOLLAND

Dutch food is of excellent quality, and the standard of service in shops excellent. You will find first-class meat, cheeses and vegetables.

There are many supermarkets, as well as small shops and markets. For names of shops see page 51.

The currency in Holland is the guilder (*gulden*) of 100 cents.

COOKING IN HOLLAND

There is a similarity between the Flemish cooking of Belgium and Dutch cuisine, but Holland also has many original dishes of its own.

The dairy produce is excellent. Holland specializes in producing early salad ingredients and vegetables of all kinds.

Because of the Dutch links with Indonesia you will find an interesting range of food from rather plain bland dishes to highly spiced ones; rice is also very popular and Chicken Jambalaya (see below) is a typical dish, adapted for campers. It can be made more interesting with the addition of various spices.

Tomatoes au Gratin

Slice 8 large tomatoes, skin if wished. Wash and slice 225g (8oz) mushrooms. Chop enough chives to give 2 tablespoons. Grate approximately 300g (10oz) Dutch Edam or Gouda cheese. Heat 25g (1oz) butter in a pan and fry the mushrooms gently for a few minutes. Put a third of the tomatoes into a dish, top with half the mushrooms, half the chives and 100g (4oz) of the cheese. Season lightly with a little salt and pepper. Add half the remaining tomatoes, all the rest of the mushrooms and chives, together with another 100g (4oz) cheese and seasoning. Top with the remaining tomatoes and cheese, together with 2–3 tablespoons soft breadcrumbs. Bake for 25 minutes in the centre of a moderate oven, 190°C, 375°F, Gas Mark 5. *Serves 4.*
To vary: Use washed, but not peeled, thinly sliced courgettes as well as, or instead of, the mushrooms.
Freezing: This freezes well for up to 3 months.

Chicken Jambalaya

This dish needs a good-sized saucepan to hold the chicken,

vegetables and rice. It makes an interesting and sustaining meal in one pan.

generous 1kg (2½–3lb) young roasting chicken with giblets	2–3 sticks celery
	2–3 rashers bacon
	300ml (½ pint) white wine
1 tablespoon oil	600ml (1 pint) water
4 onions	225g (8oz) long grain rice
4–8 carrots	salt and pepper

Wipe the chicken and the giblets, discard the neck and stomach, but use the liver and heart. Heat the oil in the saucepan and put in the chicken, breast side downwards. Heat for 5–10 minutes until slightly browned then turn, so that the breast is uppermost. Peel the onion and carrots, dice celery. De-rind and chop bacon. Put vegetables, bacon, wine, water and giblets into the saucepan and bring just to simmering point. Cover the saucepan, lower the heat and allow the liquid to continue simmering for 45 minutes. Add the rice and a little salt and pepper. Bring the liquid to the boil, stir briskly, cover the pan again, lower the heat and simmer for 15–20 minutes until the chicken and rice are tender. Lift the chicken from the pan on to a plate. Spoon the rice mixture on to a serving dish; carve or joint the chicken and place over the rice. The giblets can be chopped and mixed with the rice and vegetables. *Serves 4–6*
To vary: Add mushrooms and small or diced Frankfurter sausages just before adding the rice.
Freezing: The cooked dish should not be frozen but this is an excellent recipe in which to use a defrosted frozen chicken.

VISITING ITALY

Italy and its regions of Sicily and Sardinia are wonderful countries for visitors, who can buy the most perfect fruit, vegetables and cheeses, as well as interesting fish, good meat and excellent wines.

There are good convenience foods available. A chain of shops specializing in a whole range of excellent ready-prepared meats and other foods are now becoming very popular in many Italian towns. The name to look for is *Rosticceria*.

Currency in Italy is the *lira* (pl *lire*) of 100 centisimi.

Food shops are:

Baker	—	*Fornaio*
Butcher	—	*Macelleria*
Dairy	—	*Latteria*
Fruiterer and greengrocer	—	*Verduraio*

COOKING IN ITALY

Some of the things you will enjoy about cooking in Italy are the freshness of the ingredients you can buy, the lavish displays of fresh fruit and vegetables, the opportunity to taste real Italian pasta and the incredible variety of Italian ice creams, quite unlike any you will find elsewhere in the world.

Obviously the range of foods you can buy will vary enormously according to the region of Italy in which you are staying, but the following will give a general idea of some of the foods you can enjoy in this beautiful country.

Hors d'oeuvre

You can serve salad, cooked vegetables, smaller portions of pasta dishes or risottos for an hors d'oeuvre. The Italian antipasti is a mixed hors d'oeuvre, and you can produce this very easily from slices of Italian salami, hard-boiled eggs topped with cream cheese and cooked or raw vegetables.

Fish

The word scampi came to us from Italy, and describes the really large prawns that have become so popular throughout various countries. The simplest way to serve them if bought alive is to put them into cold water and gradually bring to the boil, adding salt to taste. This is considered the most humane way to deal with the fish. The scampi are then shelled and can be eaten in salads. They can also be heated through for a few minutes in butter and chopped fennel or parsley. Crushed garlic and lemon juice can be added to this delicious dish.

There are many other kinds of shellfish from lobster, crab and crayfish, to the more economical mussels, cockles and clams. You will find recipes using mussels on page 94.

One of the easiest of all ways of enjoying shell fish is in the form of a risotto (see pages 81–83).

Italian white fish vary appreciably from our familiar varieties, but the fish recipes in this book can be adapted to use these less familiar, but very good fish. Do not be frightened by the look of some of the fish, such as the very ugly, but excellent John Dory, sword fish and fresh tunny.

Pine nuts are used with fish in some Italian areas, and the following recipe gives an entirely new flavour to sole, or indeed any white fish.

Sole with Pine Nuts

Fry fillets of sole in butter or margarine until just tender. Add a few tablespoons white wine, a little chopped fennel, and 2–3 tablespoons pine nuts. 2–3 tablespoons sultanas can also be added, if you wish.

If you enjoy the combination of fish and nuts, on your return home you could adapt this recipe, using blanched chopped almonds or chopped walnuts.

Fresh Tunny Fish

This is excellent in hot or cold dishes. I combine the flavour of tomatoes and wine in this aromatic way of baking tunny:

Tunny and Tomato Casserole

Put 4 slices of tunny fish into an oiled casserole. Add a little salt, pepper, white wine and lemon juice to flavour. Top with a really thick layer of sliced tomatoes, blended with chopped fennel leaves, salt and pepper. Cover the casserole and bake for about 30 minutes (tunny is very solid and needs fairly long cooking) in the centre of a moderate oven, 190°C, 375°F, Gas Mark 5, or until fish and tomatoes are soft. *Serves 4*.

It is a good idea to bake more fish than you need. It is then ready to be used cold in a salad with various vegetables and mayonnaise. The casserole juices will have given it a pleasant flavour for the salad.

Cooking Pasta

When you know you are holidaying in Italy it is wise to check that the cooking equipment includes a good-sized saucepan, as this is essential for cooking pasta.

Whatever pasta you choose to cook, the same basic rules apply:-

1 Be critical about purchasing it; do not look for the cheapest pasta, select the kinds bought by the local shoppers, for, although many Italians prefer to make their own pasta, a great many busy people do not. Certainly I doubt whether you would want to do this on holiday!

The range of shapes is almost bewildering, so I have given a brief glossary on page 85, together with pasta dishes.

2 Have a sufficiently large amount of water (hence the need for a large saucepan). You need at least 1200ml (2 pints) boiling water for each 100g (4oz) pasta. Bring the water to the boil, add salt to taste before adding the pasta.

3 Keep the water boiling steadily, and strain the pasta as soon as it is cooked. The Italians have an expression '*al dente*', which means that the pasta should not be soggy, but should retain a certain amount of 'bite'.

There is no need to look for elaborate dishes, simply tip the pasta back into the saucepan, add a good knob of butter or margarine, some chopped herbs, parsley, fennel leaves, and grated cheese, and you have a splendid dish. Slightly more elaborate dishes are made by adding a little cream or the famous Italian Ricotto (cream cheese), or chopped anchovy fillets (these are often very salty, so soak in milk for a time, drain and use).

Pasta makes an excellent accompaniment to fish, meat and poultry dishes, and also means no potato peeling!

Leftover pasta can be reheated by dropping into boiling water for a few minutes and draining. I like pasta as an ingredient in really sustaining salads. Blend with mayonnaise, lots of herbs, vegetables, chopped eggs, meat or fish.

Meat and Poultry

To many people the most famous of all Italian meat dishes is a Bolognese (meat) sauce. I have given my favourite simplified recipe for this sauce on page 81, for wherever you may be in the world on holiday, I am sure you will find you can use this in various ways. It is not only an essential ingredient for topping spaghetti or risotto, but an excellent filling for an omelette, pancakes, or cannelloni – and it is usually a family favourite.

Although Italians do not consume a great deal of meat, good pork, lamb, and of course veal can be found. The beef can sometimes appear comparatively tough.

Italian chickens and turkeys are good quality. The milder-flavoured meats and poultry are often served with ham and cheese, as in the recipe immediately below. Use just the breast of a chicken for this in place of veal, and save the legs and wings for another dish. They could be fried in the pan before cooking the main recipe, and served cold in a salad.

Vitello alla Modenese

Flatten thin escalopes (slices of veal cut from the leg – often called the fillet) and coat in a little seasoned flour or cornflour, if you have this. The veal may then be coated in beaten egg and breadcrumbs, but this is not essential. Heat a generous amount of butter in a frying pan and fry the veal steadily for about 4–5 minutes on either side, or until tender. Top with slices of cooked ham, then with cheese. Select one of the many excellent Italian cheeses for this – *Bel Paese*, *Mozzarella* or *Pecorino* are excellent varieties for this dish; of course when you are cooking in other countries, substitute the best cooking cheese of that particular country. Place the frying pan under the grill and allow the cheese to melt. If the particular cooker has no grill compartment, then transfer the veal and topping to an oven-proof dish and heat for a short time in a hot oven. Serve as soon as possible with a green vegetable – peas are particularly good, or a crisp salad.

Saltimbocca

Parma ham or *proscuitto* is another excellent topping for fried veal, which is usually left uncoated in this dish. Simply place the Parma ham on top of the veal in the pan and allow another one or two minutes cooking to heat through. The authentic method of preparing this dish is called *Saltimbocca*: halve each thin slice of veal, lay the *proscuitto* on half of the pieces of veal, with a fresh sage leaf (these are easily available). Cover with the other halves, secure with a small toothpick or wooden cocktail stick, and fry until the meat is tender. In this version the meat is uncoated. A little white wine can be added towards the end of the cooking time. Lift the meat on to a dish or plates, stir the pan so the wine absorbs any butter and meat pieces, then pour over the veal.

Bolognese Sauce

Peel and finely chop 2 medium onions, 1–2 cloves of garlic, and a few mushrooms. Toss in 50g (2oz) butter or margarine or 2 tablespoons oil. Add 450g (1lb) minced beef and blend with the vegetables. Pour in 300ml (½ pint) beef stock, or water and a beef stock cube, plus a wineglass of red wine, salt and pepper to taste and 2–3 tablespoons tomato purée. Simmer gently for about 45 minutes until the meat is tender and the excess liquid has evaporated.

Taste and adjust the seasoning. Obviously this sauce can be varied; you can add chopped parsley or other herbs, like oregano, diced green or red peppers, fresh tomatoes, etc.

Serve the sauce with any pasta or risotto. *Serves 4.*

Risottos

The word *risotto* means a rice dish. These are as much a feature of Italian cooking as pasta dishes. They enable you to use small amounts of various ingredients in an appetizing and economical way. One of the great advantages of a risotto is that all the cooking is done in one saucepan.

Italian rice is of good quality, and has a pleasant translucent appearance. It does, however, tend to take longer to cook than the rice to which we are more accustomed, so naturally you must allow extra liquid. When cooking a risotto, leave the lid off the pan, to allow excess liquid to evaporate easily. The rice should be of a creamy consistency when cooking is completed, but should never be so soft or over-cooked that it loses its flavour.

The plain risotto given immediately below is ideal to serve with main dishes.

Plain Risotto

Heat 25g (1oz) butter, or a tablespoon oil, in a saucepan. Toss

225g (8oz) Italian or long grain rice (if you have brought this with you) in this. You can add a chopped onion at this stage, or a few diced tomatoes or mushrooms, to give added flavour and colour, but they are not essential.

If using Italian rice add 900ml (1½ pints) chicken stock, or water with 1 or 2 chicken stock cubes; salt to taste.

If using long grain rice, add only 600ml (1 pint) liquid.

Bring the liquid to the boil, stir briskly, lower the heat and simmer steadily until the rice is cooked, and the excess liquid has been absorbed. This takes about 25 minutes with Italian rice, but less than 20 minutes with ordinary long grain rice.

Serve the risotto topped with grated Parmesan. *Serves 4–6.*

Risotto alla Marinara

For this sea food dish, an interesting selection of cooked shell fish is added to the rice mixture towards the end of the cooking time. A pinch of powdered saffron, or a few saffron strands, added to the liquid gives the rice an attractive yellow colour.

Risotto alla Finanziera

Minced or finely diced meat can be cooked with the butter, and a classic example is this famous liver dish. Heat 75g (3oz) butter, or 3 tablespoons oil, and fry approximately 100g (4oz) sliced mushrooms and 6–8 diced chicken livers in this, together with 1 or 2 finely chopped onions. Add the rice and continue as the plain risotto; you may need a little extra liquid. Finely diced red or green pepper could also be added if desired.

Any leftover cooked meat can be finely diced and added to the rice mixture towards the end of the cooking time. *Serves 4–6.*

Risotto al Salta

This literally means a somersault risotto and it is a splendid way of using up leftover risottos. Heat a little butter in a pan, and add the rice mixture, which will have become firm as it cooled. Fry on one side until golden brown, then somersault (turn upside down) on to a plate. You can serve it at once, or heat a little more butter in the pan and slide the mixture back again into the pan to crisp and brown on the other side. Top with grated cheese and serve with a green salad.

Oven-cooked Risotto

It may be more convenient to cook the risottos in the oven, as they can then be left unattended. Use the same basic recipe, but be a little more generous with the liquid. Allow a deep dish, so there is no fear of the liquid boiling over before the rice begins to absorb it. Cover tightly with a lid or foil and leave cooking, just as you would a rice pudding, in the coolest part of a very slow oven, about 140°C, 275°F, Gas Mark 1 for about 2 hours.

It is an advantage if you can heat the butter or oil in the dish first, and turn the rice and other ingredients in this, so they have a chance to absorb it before you add the liquid.

Vegetarians can make the most delicious vegetable risottos with finely diced uncooked vegetables, or by adding cooked vegetables to the rice just before serving. Omit the chicken stock and use water with a little more onion or other well-flavoured vegetables.

Rice Salad

A leftover risotto makes an excellent ingredient for a salad. Blend with a little oil and vinegar while still warm. Allow the rice to cool, then blend with diced raw vegetables. Choose those with a firm texture to make a contrast to the softness of the rice. Fish or meat can also be added.

Vegetables

Italian vegetables are of an incredible variety, many familiar, but of superb quality; but some predominate in national specialities:

Aubergines are first class. Their flavour can be enjoyed at its best if you simply slice and fry them. Coat each thin slice in seasoned flour or cornflour, if you have it, then fry in hot oil for several minutes, until crisp and brown, on both sides. (See the information about aubergines on page 73.)

Fennel is probably the outstanding vegetable in Italy. The bulb (often called the head) is white and plump, and can be cooked or eaten raw in salads. It has a definite aniseed taste, and a crisp texture when eaten raw, which most people find enjoyable. The feathery green leaves are chopped and added to sauces, or used as a garnish. They are particularly good with fish.

One way to cook fennel is to put the whole head into boiling salted water, boil for about 15 minutes, or until nearly softened, then drain and slice. Put the slices into a dish with a little cream and grated cheese, and bake in the oven until the cheese just melts. Fennel can also be fairly finely chopped before being cooked in salted boiling water, then drained and tossed in melted butter and chopped parsley.

I also like it cooked in a fresh tomato purée: simmer skinned and chopped tomatoes, with a little finely chopped peeled onion and garlic. When the tomatoes have formed a purée, dilute it with a little water to make a thinner mixture, then add thickly sliced uncooked fennel, and simmer for 12–15 minutes, or until just tender. Do not overcook the vegetable; always retain a little of the firm texture.

Peppers

Sweet peppers, often called capsicums, are used in most countries, but you will find superb quality peppers in many parts of Italy. Use these peppers (green, yellow or red, but all equally delicious) in salads, or add to various savoury dishes. If you dislike the skins, put the peppers into the oven, or under the grill for a few minutes, until the outer thin skin breaks and strip it away. The peppers can be stuffed in various ways. The following is a typical Italian dish:

Anchovy Peppers

Cut a slice from the stalk end of 4 peppers, discard the core and seeds from the rest of the pepper, but keep them a good shape. If you like a slightly softened texture, simmer the whole peppers, plus the slices removed, in boiling salted water for 5 minutes, then drain. If you prefer a firmer texture, omit this stage. Chop 4–6 large tomatoes, put into a saucepan with 1–2 peeled and crushed garlic cloves and 1 tablespoon olive oil; add a shake of pepper, but no salt. Simmer until you have a thick purée, then add 6–8 chopped anchovy fillets. Put into the peppers and replace the 'lids' (slices). Bake for about 25 minutes in the centre of a moderate oven, 180°C, 350°F, Gas Mark 4. *Serves 4*.

This, of course, is only one of the many ways in which the peppers can be filled. On page 116 is a recipe for raw stuffed peppers, which would be excellent with Italian Ricotto (cream cheese).

Zucchini

This is the Italian name of the vegetable we generally call courgettes. There are several recipes using courgettes in this book, for they are an easy-to-prepare and popular vegetable. Always wash courgettes well, as they are not peeled before cooking.

One very easy supper dish is to slice about 450g (1lb) courgettes very thinly (discard the tough ends), then cook the slices in 75g (3oz) butter or margarine until soft, stirring frequently so the slices do not burn. Add 4 eggs, a few tablespoons milk, and a little salt and pepper. Stir over a low heat until the eggs are nearly set, then add a few spoonfuls of grated cheese. Serve with fresh bread as soon as cooked. *Serves 4*.

Some Pasta Shapes

Cannelloni – large tubes to fill with Bolognese sauce, chopped ham blended with cream cheese, spinach. Usually topped with cheese sauce.
Fusilli – a twisted macaroni, cook and serve with main dishes.
Lasagne – a wide ribbon noodle, serve layered with Bolognese and cheese sauces.
Ravioli – square of pasta with a filling.
Rigatoni – a ribbed cannelloni.
Spaghetti – the long pasta we all know.

Simple Savouries

The Italian Pizza has now become a world-famous dish, but you will be able to buy a large variety of these ready-made.

There is another kind of quick savoury at which the Italians excel, a kind of fried sandwich called 'cheese in a carriage'. This is made by sandwiching slices of cheese and ham in bread and butter, coating them in beaten egg, then fine breadcrumbs, and frying until crisp and brown. A simpler version is the French

Croque-Monsieur in which the sandwiches are just dipped in beaten egg, then shallow fried in butter.

Sandwiches filled with cheese and anchovy fillets and fried are another typical Italian snack. Continental anchovies are often much more salty than those we buy in cans, so do soak them in milk for a while before using them, then drain well. (Do not use the leftover milk except to add to a sauce with fish.) These cheese and anchovy sandwiches need not be dipped in egg or coated, but are simply fried in hot butter or fat until the bread is crisp on either side. You can add sliced tomatoes to the cheese and anchovies for extra flavour and colour in the middle of the crisp sandwich.

Using Pasta

Top cooked pasta with Bolognese sauce (see the recipe on page 81).

Mix cooked pasta with chopped fennel and chopped hard-boiled eggs.

Stir a selection of cooked shell fish into hot cooked pasta.

Stir chopped fried bacon or cooked ham with chopped fried onions and chopped parsley into cooked pasta.

Desserts

You will be able to choose from a huge array of pastries and cream cakes, together with the unequalled variety of Italian ice creams.

One very simple, but delicious dessert, that blends well with ripe soft fruits, is world famous and almost ridiculously simple. It is doubtful whether you will have double saucepans, but a basin, perched securely over a pan of hot, but not boiling, water is just as good:

Zabaglione

Put the yolks of 3–4 eggs and 75g (3oz) sugar into the basin over the hot water and whisk until thick and creamy. Gradually whisk in 150ml (¼ pint) Marsala. Serve warm by itself, or spooned over soft fruit. *Serves 4, or 6 with fruit.*

Chocolate Mousse

The leftover egg whites can be used up in a simple chocolate mousse. Simply melt about 100g (4oz) chocolate in a basin over hot water and leave to cool, but do not allow to set again. Whisk the 3–4 egg whites until stiff; if you like very sweet desserts whisk in 25g (1oz) sugar, then fold into the melted chocolate. Spoon into dishes or glasses and chill slightly, but eat while freshly made. *Serves 4.*

Cheese and Fruit

The delicious cream and curd cheeses can be served with fresh figs, pears, peaches or melon, as a dessert.

VISITING MALTA

In the island of Malta you will find an interesting blending of Italian and Portuguese food. There are many pasta and rice dishes. Because of past links with Britain, British fare is well known too.

The kind of recipes given under *Cooking in Italy* will also be suitable for holiday cooking in Malta.

The currency is the Maltese pound (£M).

COOKING IN MALTA

Pot roasting is a popular cooking method in Malta. It is the best way to cook meat if you have no oven. It is also ideal if the meat is a bit tough, so good for slightly cheaper cuts of beef, mutton rather than lamb, and for older chickens.

Brown the meat in the bottom of a large pan. If the flesh is very lean, as with chicken, add a little fat. When browned, remove from the pan and pour away any surplus fat. Put a layer of vegetables into the pan; keep these large so they retain their shape in cooking. Choose potatoes (washed and in their skins), carrots, turnips, etc. Vegetables that need only a short cooking time can be added later. Cover the vegetables with water, or use a little inexpensive wine. Season to taste. Replace the meat on the bed of vegetables, making sure it is not covered in liquid. Put the lid on the pan, making sure it fits well – wedge it with a piece of foil if necessary. Simmer gently, allowing approximately 40–45 minutes per 450g (1lb) for meat, or about 30 minutes per 450g (1lb) for chicken if reasonably tender. The liquid at the bottom of the pan makes a good gravy.

VISITING MOROCCO

This country is developing as a place in which you can cater for yourself in camps or holiday flats.

I have not given the names of shops as they would be in Arabic and therefore difficult to read, but undoubtedly the best place to shop in any town in Morocco is in the market, which sells magnificent fruit and vegetables of all kinds as well as good quality fish and meat.

While one is expected to bargain for other shopping, food prices are firmly fixed and displayed in the markets!

The currency of Morocco is the dirham (DH) of 100 francs.

COOKING IN MOROCCO

With the wide range of food in most areas, cooking should not be a problem. Most people associate Morocco with cous-cous, a meat and vegetable dish based upon coarse semolina, not unlike rice. This is time-consuming to prepare yourself, so enjoy it in specialist restaurants.

Invest in long metal skewers and make kebabs, Arabic-style. The diced tender meat should be brushed with melted butter and sprinkled with chopped dried herbs and spice before cooking. Garam-masala is the usual spice; this is a combination of many flavours, including curry and ginger, and is fairly hot. Cook the kebabs over a camp fire, under a grill, or even in an oven.

Sis Köfta

These are small meat balls, cooked on skewers. Blend 350g (12oz) minced mutton, salt, pepper, a little onion juice (made by leaving grated onion to stand, then pouring off the juice) and 1 or 2 eggs to bind. Take small amounts, mould into balls and secure on oiled skewers; cook as kebabs. *Serves 4.*

Kefta Sauce

Serve this traditional *Kefta* sauce with meat dishes. Skin and chop 4 tomatoes,. peel and grate an onion and crush 1–2 cloves of garlic. Put the vegetables into a pan with 2–3 tablespoons oil, a pinch of salt, a shake of cayenne pepper, a pinch of ground ginger, 300ml (½ pint) water, approximately 1 tablespoon chopped parsley and a little chopped mint. Simmer until you have a thick purée. *Serves 4.*

Lemon Chicken

Chicken, whether boiled or roasted, acquires a new flavour if lavishly sprinkled with lemon juice before cooking. The lemon halves, with the pips removed, can be put into the cavity of the bird.

VISITING NORWAY

The shopping in this beautiful country is mostly done in supermarkets; even small grocers tend to operate on a self-service basis. Supermarkets are often marked *Dagligvarer* (translated this means daily wares), and you will also find the names *Samvirkelaget*, *Domus* and *S laget*.

You will be able to buy wonderful fresh fish, a large range of ready-prepared salads, cooked meats, ready-prepared stews, and ingredients for open sandwiches.

Another helpful shop is the *Gatekjøkken*, where one can buy take-away hot food.

Alcohol is only obtainable from State monopoly shops. These keep ordinary shop hours, and are named *Vinmonopolet.*

The currency in Norway is the Norwegian *krone* (Kr) of 100 øre.

The shops from which you can buy food are:

Baker   — *Baker* or *Konditori*
Butcher   — *Slakteri* or *Kjøtthandler*
Dairy   — No dairies*, ask for *Melk* in
                                  supermarket
Fishmonger   — *Fiskehandler* or *Fisketorvet*.
                                  There are splendid fish
                                  markets in coastal areas.
Fruiterer and greengrocer   — *Frukthandler* or *Gronnsaker*
Grocer   — Mostly confined to one or two
                                  tea and coffee shops, but
                                  called *Kolonial*, if you can find
                                  them.

*A few country districts have dairies – called *Meieriet*.

COOKING IN NORWAY

The dishes on pages 95–100 are typically Scandinavian and suitable for preparation in this country. You will also be able to enjoy open sandwiches (see page 56), and some of the freshest fish you have ever tasted. There are fish dishes under *Cooking in Finland*, on page 58.

Cheese in Scandinavia

Cheese is an important ingredient in Scandinavian meals. You may be surprised to see people eating this with crispbread or rye bread and butter at the start, rather than the end, of the meal.

Denmark produces a whole range of good cheeses, from the famous Danish Blue, to Havarti, Danbo (plain or with caraway seeds), Samsoe etc. There is a very unusual cheese you should try in Norway called *Gjetøst*; this has a strange sweet flavour and will appeal to children who do not like ordinary cheese.

VISITING PORTUGAL

If you have never been to Portugal before you will be surprised at the differences in food and living habits between Portugal and Spain. Although so near, they are quite different.

The currency in Portugal is the *escudo* of 100 *centavos*.

COOKING IN PORTUGAL

Many of the fish dishes throughout this book will be useful when in this country, for the fish is splendid. Do not miss the sardines though; freshly-caught sardines are a treat. Flavour the fish with chopped onions and tomatoes when you fry them, or sprinkle with lemon juice and chopped herbs when you grill them. Always cook extra for they can be used cold in salads; there is a recipe on page 110.

Add a little port wine when frying meat; it gives a wonderful richness to chops or steaks.

Oranges are very plentiful. For an unusual, but almost ridiculously simple dessert, bake them in their skins; allow approximately 30 minutes in a moderate oven, 180°C, 350°F, Gas Mark 4. Halve the cooked oranges and top with a little sugar and wine.

VISITING SPAIN

Spain has become the most popular of all holiday countries. Shopping for foods is easy in most areas, and in the Balearic and Canary Islands. Ready-prepared foods are often available in a *charcuteria*, or in some restaurants.

Currency in Spain is the *peseta* (ptas) of 100 *céntimos*.

Food shops are:

Supermarket (selling good range of foods)	— *Supermercado*, or *Tienda de Comestibles*, *Tienda de Alimentacion*, *ultramarinos*.
General markets (selling good range of foods)	— *el Mercado* *La Plaza*
Fish market	— *Mercado de Pescado*
Baker	— *Panaderia*
Butcher	— *Carniceria*
Dairy	— *Lecheria*
Fishmonger	— *Pescaderia*
Fruiterer and greengrocer	— *Fruteria* and *Verduleria*

If you want to buy alcohol, the name to look for is *Bodega*.

COOKING IN SPAIN

The cooking in Spain is as colourful as the country. Oil is usually used as a cooking medium. There is no truth in the belief that food cooked in oil tends to be greasy. Well-fried food cooked properly in oil is dry in texture and delicious, for oil can be heated to a good temperature without fear of it burning.

Tomatoes, peppers, nuts, rice and olives are some of the ingredients you will see used a great deal.

Tapas and Hors d'oeuvre

These are the Spanish 'nibbles' that are served before the meal. If you have been out for a drink, before returning home to prepare for the main meal, you may well have feasted so generously on these that an hors d'oeuvre is unnecessary. You can serve your own *Tapas*, made from small portions of fish and meat with olives and tiny pieces of vegetable to garnish.

There are, however, a number of speedy dishes you could prepare for the start of a meal.

Many of these are based upon eggs, of which Spanish cooks have produced a number of excellent dishes, the most famous of all being a Spanish omelette or *Tortilla*. This of course is an ideal dish for a main meal, with more generous portions.

Many cooks avow that the true *Tortilla* has just cooked potatoes and onions as the basic flavouring, but of course this can be adjusted to the ingredients available. This is how the basic omelette is made:

Tortilla

Dice cooked or well-drained canned potatoes. Peel and thinly slice or chop onions. Use about 1 medium potato and ½–1 medium onion to each 2 eggs. Fry the onions in oil, or a little butter and oil, until nearly tender, add the potatoes and heat thoroughly. Beat the eggs with a little salt and pepper, you can add about ½ egg shell of water to each egg to give a lighter result. Pour the beaten eggs over the hot vegetables and cook until set, tilting the pan, so the liquid egg runs to the sides.

A *Tortilla* is served without folding. It is interesting that this is also considered a good cold dish for a packed meal, so remember this when packing food for a picnic.

To vary the Tortilla you can heat cooked shell fish, diced ham, the Spanish spiced *Choriza* (sausage) or other cooked vegetables in the oil or butter. If you feel that the mixture is a little rich with all the ingredients fried first in oil, then simmer these in water or stock, drain well and mix with the eggs, then cook the omelette in the usual way.

Scrambled Eggs

Scrambled eggs can be flavoured with chopped olives, or shell fish can be added or heated in the butter before adding the eggs. Another favourite dish is cooked rice blended with eggs, and scrambled very lightly. You can add chopped green pepper, chopped mushrooms, and peeled and chopped onion, to the rice when cooking this.

Eggs in Nests

An egg dish that is particularly popular with children, because it looks as good as it tastes, its proper name is *Huevos al Nido*.

Cut fairly thick slices of bread, allowing one per person. Scoop out a hollow in the centre of each slice, large enough to take an egg yolk; do not scoop out so deep you break the bread. Moisten the hollowed-out part (the 'nest') with a little cream or milk and leave for a few minutes to soften, then drop a small piece of butter, about the size of a pea, into this.

Take one egg per person and separate the yolk from the white. Carefully lower the yolk into the 'nest'. Whisk the egg white until stiff, add a pinch of salt and pepper, and spoon this around and over the yolk to cover the yolk completely.

Heat a little oil or fat in a frying pan and carefully slide the bread into this, savoury meringue side uppermost. Fry steadily until the bottom of the bread is crisp and the filling just set.

An easier way to cook these is to grease a flat oven-proof dish and heat this in the oven for a short time, so the bread does not stick; put the savoury slices on to this, and bake for about 10 minutes in a moderately hot oven, 200°C, 400°F, Gas Mark 6 until the bread crisps slightly, and the meringue is golden coloured.

Gazpacho

You cannot visit Spain without tasting their chilled tomato soup called *Gazpacho*. You will probably want to make it for yourself, for it is uniquely refreshing in the Spanish heat. Normally this is based upon a smooth tomato purée, as below, but you can use canned tomato juice, or thin canned tomato soup, to save time.

Skin 450g (1lb) tomatoes, chop finely, pound, sieve or liquidize. Peel and chop a medium onion, about ¼ of a cucumber, and ¼–½ a green pepper and blend with the tomato purée. Add oil (classic recipes use 2–3 tablespoons olive oil) and enough ice cold water to give a flowing consistency. Season well and chill. Serve with more diced onion, cucumber, green pepper and bread. *Serves 4.*

Paella

This famous 'meal in a pan' is easily made. I am not giving quantities; these depend on personal taste. Cut up a raw young chicken and fry in a little oil; add several tablespoons rice and toss in the oil. Cover with plenty of stock, or water and a stock cube. Simmer until the chicken and rice are nearly tender, then add shell fish of all kinds with frozen peas and chopped herbs. Season well and complete the cooking.

Cooking Mussels

Mussels are to be found in most countries and they are used in a great variety of ways. Cooked mussels can be added to the Paella above. The first thing is to wash the mussels well and check upon their freshness. To do this tap each one sharply. Any that do not close must be discarded. Put the mussels into a large pan, with water or wine to cover, add a bunch of herbs, 1 or 2 peeled chopped onions, salt and pepper. Heat steadily only until the shells open – too much cooking toughens the fish. Pull away one shell and discard any fish that have not opened. Serve the fish with the liquid as the French *Moules Marinière* or the Spanish *Mejillonés*.

You can adapt this by adding chopped tomatoes to the cooking liquid, or butter or cream to finish when the mussels are open, or you can thicken the liquid.

VISITING SWEDEN

You can plan a holiday in Sweden for winter sports or for summer activities. Shopping will be interesting and easy, as the standard of living in this country is very high.

You will be able to buy a variety of cooked meats, and other take-away food, from delicatessen counters.

Wines, spirits and beers may only be purchased from the state-owned shops, known as *Systembolaget*.

Most towns have good food markets.

Currency in Sweden is the Swedish *krona* (SKr) of 100 öre.

Food shops are:

Baker	—	*Bagare*
Butcher	—	*Slaktare*
Dairy	—	*Mjölk affär*, but there are very few dairies left in Sweden nowadays – buy from supermarkets.
Fruiterer and greengrocer	—	*Frukt handlare*
Grocer	—	*Specerie handlare*

COOKING IN SCANDINAVIA

Do try and have one or two meals in a restaurant in Scandinavia so that you can admire the presentation of the food. Cooks and chefs in all these countries have perfected the art of garnishing food beautifully and I am sure you will pick up some very good tips for home.

Open sandwiches are a feature of all Scandinavian menus, I have mentioned these on page 56 when introducing Danish food. They are admirable fare for holiday-makers, as they are easily-made, sustaining and interesting.

Meat is expensive, but you can obtain excellent cooked meats for cold buffets.

Hors d'oeuvre and Soups

The smoked fish that are so much part of a Scandinavian cold table – smoked eel, mackerel or salmon – make the easiest hors d'oeuvre. They are invariably served with scrambled egg.

Or try some of the unusual herring dishes that you can obtain ready-prepared. There are salt herrings in various kinds of dressings, for example curry or onion-flavoured, or you can buy the salt herring ready to dice and blend with other foods. The following is a typical salad based on this most popular Scandinavian fish. These herrings are really very salty, so can be soaked in a little milk before using.

Scandinavian Herring Salad

Dice 2 salt herrings, blend with several diced cold potatoes, a diced medium cooked beetroot, 2 diced dessert apples, and a few diced gherkins or a portion of pickled cucumber.

Blend with a cream dressing made by mixing 4–5 tablespoons double cream with 2 tablespoons vinegar, a shake of pepper and 1–1½ tablespoons sugar. Pour over the fish mixture. Spoon on to a bed of lettuce or parsley. Garnish with sliced hard-boiled eggs and chopped dill. Serve with crispbread. *Serves 4–6.*

Dill is a herb that is used extensively, not only on fish dishes, but over cooked potatoes or with boiled lamb.

Fish Soup

Put approximately 450g (1lb) cod into a saucepan. Add 2–3 chopped sticks of celery, 1–2 peeled and quartered onions. Pour on just over 600ml (1 pint) water with salt and pepper to taste. Bring the liquid to simmering point, cover the pan and simmer gently for 15 minutes. Either strain the liquid or, if easier, remove the fish, celery and onions with a spoon, then pour the liquid into a basin.

Heat 50g (2oz) butter or margarine in the saucepan, add 50g (2oz) flour and stir for 2–3 minutes. Some recipes allow this mixture to turn golden but do not let it burn. Blend in 300ml (½ pint) milk and the fish stock, bring to the boil and allow to cook for about 5 minutes, stirring or whisking until very smooth. Break the fish into small pieces and return to the liquid, together with a few cooked peeled prawns. *Serves 6.*
Note. The leftover vegetables can be used in a salad or with a main dish.

Fish Cream Soup

This is made from fish stock, the liquid used when poaching fish. There is no fish in the soup although the liquid is prepared as for Fish Soup (see previous recipe), but cream is added for extra flavour.

Fruit Soups

These are a feature of Scandinavian cookery and they are very popular. You can buy packet versions, but these soups are easily made from the fresh ingredients.

Use fairly acid fruits, such as peeled, diced apples, whole cherries, diced rhubarb or rather sharp-flavoured plums. Simmer in water, with a little sugar, as though you were cooking fruit for a dessert, but allow the fruit to become really soft and use more liquid. Flavour the soup with a little white wine or ground spice, such as cinnamon. Serve this hot or cold.

Some recipes are thickened with cornflour, potato flour or tapioca, but personally I think the soup is more refreshing if left unthickened. You can add a little dried fruit if desired. Remember it *is* a soup and should be refreshing and not over-sweetened. *To vary*: If you are in a country district, gather blueberries or rose hips for a traditional fruit soup.

Meat

Scandinavian meat dishes are similar to classic meat dishes, except in the flavourings used.

Cook lamb with mixed vegetables, but flavour the liquid with dill, rather than other herbs, following the French recipe for Navarin of Lamb on page 65. The Scandinavians have developed their own version of a hamburger, which they call a Lindström cake or Beef à la Lindström. A simple recipe for these follows.

Beef à la Lindström

Blend approximately 450g (1lb) good quality raw minced beef with approximately 100g (4oz) very finely diced cooked potato and the same amount of finely diced cooked beetroot. Add a little chopped onion, a few capers (if available), salt, pepper and 1–2 egg yolks to bind. Sometimes a little cream is added too. Pound together until smooth. Make into small cakes and fry in butter. *Serves 4*.

Fish Dishes

In addition to familiar fish such as cod, fresh haddock, herring and mackerel, you will find peculiarly Scandinavian methods of treating fish, such as *Lutefisk* (this is the spelling in Norway, it is similar but not identical in other countries, i.e. *Lipeäkala* in Finland and *Lutfisk* in Sweden).

This is made by curing cod or ling. It is a speciality for the Christmas period, so you will find it in the supermarket or fish suppliers if you are visiting any of the Scandinavian countries for winter sports.

The fish can be boiled or baked. If you only have aluminium saucepans it is better to bake it in foil as the curing process is affected by some metals and the fish may discolour.

Serve with a white sauce, to which extra butter and cream is added for richness.

To make a generous amount of sauce for 4 people heat 50g (2oz) butter in a saucepan, stir in 25g (1oz) flour, then gradually add 300ml (½ pint) milk and 150ml (¼ pint) double cream. Bring to the boil, stirring all the time, and cook until slightly thickened. Add a sparing amount of salt, but a generous shake of pepper. You can also add a little ground allspice.

The luxury fish of Scandinavia, apart from shell fish, is salmon. For special occasions you may be able to buy the traditional salted salmon, known as *lax*; this is worth trying as an alternative to smoked salmon, for it has an interesting, sweet-sour flavour. It is, however, just as costly as smoked salmon. Serve *lax* as an hors d'oeuvre, or with a salad for a main course. It is usually served with a mustard sauce (see recipe opposite).

Serve grilled or baked herrings or mackerel with a fairly sharp apple purée. This makes a good, tart accompaniment to these oily fish.

Fish balls and fish pudding are available ready-made (the former are sold in cans), and only require heating. These excellent fish dishes look very white and uninspiring but taste delicious. Heat canned fish balls in the liquid from the can, drain, serve with melted butter. Fry fish balls or slices of fish pudding in hot butter or margarine.

A whole fish pudding can be steamed over a little water for about 45 minutes, then served with butter and chopped herbs.

There are many complex fish dishes associated with Scandinavia. But I am sure you will want to avoid dishes that are too time-consuming, and the superb quality of the fish is shown to advantage when cooked simply.

Baked Fish

To save washing up, wrap the well-seasoned fish in buttered foil and bake until tender. The time will vary according to the thickness of the fish, as well as the weight. Allow about 25 minutes in a moderate oven, 190°C, 375°F, Gas Mark 5, for 450g (1lb) fairly thin cod fillet. It is better to under-estimate the timing than to over-cook the fish. Have the join of the foil parcel loosely folded, so that it is easy to open this (be careful, there is a lot of steam) and inspect the fish.
To vary: Add sliced tomatoes or sliced mushrooms and chopped herbs to flavour the fish.

Fried Fish

Do not bother to coat the fish but simply fry in a generous amount of butter or margarine and serve with lemon and chopped dill.

Poached Fish

Simmer the fish in a little water with sprigs of dill or parsley and salt and pepper to taste. Lift from the liquid and serve with a generous amount of melted butter, or melted butter and lemon juice. This is a suitable method of preparation for most fish.

Scandinavians also serve mayonnaise with hot fish, which is a very simple way of providing a sauce.

Mustard Sauce

Heat 1–2 tablespoons sugar with 1 tablespoon vinegar until the sugar has dissolved. Cool and blend with 1 tablespoon French mustard, 2–3 tablespoons salad oil (taste as you add this, to make sure it is not too oily for your personal taste). Lastly add some finely chopped dill.

This sauce is good with *lax* or cooked fresh herrings or fresh mackerel.

Scandinavian Cold Table

You should try and plan a cold table while on holiday in Scandinavia. Obviously you will not wish to stock up with such a wide range of foods as is usual for this, but have some kind of fish, including prepared herrings, liver pâté, cold meats, salads and cheeses.

VISITING SWITZERLAND

Whether you decide to visit Switzerland for winter sports, or to enjoy the magnificent scenery and summer weather, you will find a good variety of all kinds of food readily available.

Currency in Switzerland is the Swiss *franc* (Sfr) with 50 *centimes* (or Rappen) to ½ Sfr.

Food shops may be indicated in either French or German, depending upon the region in which you are staying.

Food shops are:

	German	French
Baker	— *Bäckerei*	*Boulangerie*
Butcher	— *Metzgerei*	*Boucherie*
Dairy	— *Molkerei*	*Cremerie*
Fruiterer and green-grocer	— *Gemüse*	*Légumes**
Grocer	— *Lebensmittel*	*Epicerie*

*This is the sign often found over the shop, or occasionally you may find *Marchand de légumes*, or *Fruitier*.

COOKING IN SWITZERLAND

The national dishes vary with the area, so you will find Austrian-German type of food, as well as Italian and French dishes. One cannot however ignore the most famous of all Swiss dishes, a fondue. You may be lucky enough to have been provided with a fondue heater.

Fondue

Grate 450g (1lb) cheese, either all Gruyère or a mixture of Gruyère and Emmenthal. Put into the buttered fondue pot; if there are both earthenware and metal fondue pots to choose from, select the former as it does not get so hot.

Add 300ml (½ pint) dry white wine; if you have any cornflour blend 1 teaspoon of this with the wine, for it helps to prevent the mixture curdling. Add a very little salt and pepper. Heat gently until the cheese melts. The cooking process can be started on an ordinary cooker, then the pot can be transferred to the fondue heater as the cheese begins to melt.

Serve the creamy hot cheese mixture with squares of toasted or fresh bread, speared on to forks for dipping. You can also heat small cooked sausages, squares of cooked meat or diced very tender raw steak in the delicious cheese mixture. *Serves 4–6.*

SELF-CATERING AT HOME

This chapter has been written for those of you who are holidaying in Britain or are not going away.

To busy people who spend a lot of time away from the house, a holiday at home can be most enjoyable – time to relax, time to read, to garden, and to do the various jobs for which there never normally seems enough time. But for the cook of the family, the holiday at home can be no holiday at all, unless the routine is very different from usual.

It is surprising how many unusual and fascinating things there are to do and see in practically every part of the country. Plan what to do throughout the holiday period, so each day has something special to anticipate with pleasure. There may be special events, such as a race meeting, a trip to the sea or a stately home to visit.

Consider how to keep everyone well fed with the minimum of effort and maximum of enjoyment, to fit in with the holiday mood. If your gas or electric cooker has an automatic timing device, make full use of this.

Convenience foods may be a little more expensive than basic fresh foods, but they do save time and effort.

Many dishes can be prepared before the holiday period and frozen. Having dishes from various countries from time to time brings some of the flavour of these countries into your home.

Cakes to Carry
The following recipes are all for cakes that keep well (if your

family will allow this!). You can bake them before the holiday and carry them in the car. Pack in foil, polythene or tin boxes to keep them airtight.

Traditional Fruit Cake

Cream together 175g (6oz) butter or margarine, 175g (6oz) light or dark moist brown sugar, 2 *level* tablespoons black treacle or golden syrup. Gradually beat in 4 large eggs, add 225g (8oz) plain flour sifted with 1 level teaspoon baking powder, or 125g* (4oz) self-raising and 100g (4oz) plain flour, 450g (1lb) mixed dried fruit, 50–100g (2–4oz) quartered glacé cherries, 50g (2oz) chopped blanched almonds, and 50g (2oz) chopped candied peel. Do not add any liquid. Line a 20–22cm (8–8½in) cake tin with greased greaseproof paper, put in the mixture and spread flat on top. Bake in the centre of a very moderate oven, 160°C, 325°F, Gas Mark 3, for 1 hour, then lower the heat to 150°C, 300°F, Gas Mark 2, a slow oven, for a further 1¼–1½ hours, or until the cake is firm to the touch and no longer gives a humming sound. Allow to cool in the tin and do not pull away the paper; it makes the cake firmer to carry.
*This metrication gives the best result.

To vary: For **Orange Cake** Use fine-cut marmalade plus the finely grated rind of 2 oranges in place of treacle or syrup. Use light moist brown sugar. Add only 225g (8oz) sultanas instead of mixed dried fruit; omit the cherries and almonds, but add 225g (8oz) chopped candied orange peel.

Cherry Almond Cake

Cream 175g (6oz) butter or margarine with 175g (6oz) caster sugar, gradually beat in 4 large eggs. Add either 225g (8oz) plain flour sifted with 1 teaspoon baking powder, or 125g* (4oz) plain and 100g (4oz) self-raising flour, 50g (2oz) ground almonds and 175g (6oz) quartered glacé cherries. Line a 20–22cm (8–8½in) tin with greased greaseproof paper, put in the mixture and smooth flat on top. Bake in the centre of a very moderate oven, 160°C, 325°F, Gas Mark 3, for an hour, then in a slow oven, 150°C, 300°F, Gas Mark 2 for 30–45 minutes or until firm to the

touch. This cake does not rise dramatically, but has an exceptionally moist texture.
*This metrication gives the best results.

Foods in Britain

When spending your holiday in an unfamiliar part of Britain, take the opportunity to sample the local fare. In spite of the fact that large supermarkets tend to stock the same kind of foods throughout the country, you will find some of the really traditional and specialist dishes and foods are still available. The best places to find these are in small family bakers and grocers, and in farm shops; the popularity of these has grown during the last few years.

Many farms or smallholdings advertize their own vegetables and fruits for sale; if you are feeling energetic, you will often be able to pick your own.

IN ENGLAND

The different regions in England vary quite appreciably in their special regional foods and dishes.

If you are in the West Country then clotted Devonshire or Cornish cream is not to be missed. You will be able to buy the scone-like soft rolls known as splits; although really meant as an accompaniment to cream and jam, they make an excellent breakfast roll, particularly when heated.

Saffron-flavoured cakes are still made. They have a fairly dry texture, and you may enjoy them more spread with butter.

Everywhere you will be able to buy pasties – small and large – the quality of which varies enormously. You will need to experiment, for a really perfect Cornish pasty, with good pastry and a moist filling of tender meat and vegetables, is too good to miss.

Mackerel are one of the local fish, and if you have never tasted *really fresh* mackerel before, you are in for a treat. There are recipes using mackerel on pages 69, 70 and 114.

In the Midlands and North of England you will find butcher's shops still making old-fashioned meat dishes like faggots and haslet. Both of these minced meat products are highly seasoned and just need warming in the oven. If you have no oven, wrap them in foil, put into a small quantity of water, and steam for a short time. Pease pudding is the traditional accompaniment to faggots, and it is a satisfying vegetable dish; if you cannot buy this, cook fresh, frozen or tinned peas until a soft purée. You may also find real home-made raised pies, such as the famous Melton Mowbray (pork) pie.

The Lake District not only provides fabulous scenery, but also some specialist foods, such as Cumberland sausage, a long, highly-seasoned sausage, quite unlike any other, which is cooked and then sliced. The cakes, bread and scones in many shops still have a home-made flavour. Grasmere shortbread is one excellent biscuit-like cake. Rum butter, a blending of rum, butter and brown sugar, is not only an accompaniment to Christmas pudding, but a luxury spread for bread and scones.

The magnificent Yorkshire dales are wonderful places for touring. With luck you will find real York ham and, in the bakers shops, true Yorkshire parkin and gingerbreads. If you are in Yorkshire in the game season, and feeling extravagant, you may be able to buy pheasant or grouse – a simple casserole recipe is on page 119.

Look out for locally-made cheeses, their flavour is quite different from mass-produced ones.

Smoked and Fresh Fish

As an island, Britain has a wonderful supply of fresh fish.

If you are near the East coast you must buy kippers – the cooking method suggested below avoids the caravan, tent or kitchen smelling of fish. In most coastal districts, or in the Isle of Man, shell fish should be plentiful and very fresh.

The old-fashioned method of 'jugging' cooks kippers with hardly any smell. Find a fairly large container, put in the kippers, pour over boiling water to cover, then put a lid or cloth or foil over the container and leave for 5 minutes. The kippers will be cooked and the smell hardly noticeable.

Other special fish to try and find are the tiny scallops (often called 'Queenies') in the Isle of Man and in the Channel Islands. These are delicious fried in hot butter or with bacon. They are cooked when the flesh turns white.

Smoked trout, split and filled with mixed vegetables in a horseradish-flavoured mayonnaise, becomes an exotic main dish, with no cooking needed at all.

IN IRELAND

All dairy produce is good in this beautiful green country, with its lush pastures.

Bacon and pork are specialities.

Irish soda bread is still one of their delicious foods. You will find this in all bakers and small shops. Usually round and flat, it is as light as a feather. If you want to make your own, you will find a recipe given below. The flour is mixed with buttermilk, the liquid left after taking the cream for butter and cheese. This is fairly easy to buy in Ireland, but ordinary milk can be substituted. Try also the traditional scones and oat cakes.

Look out for the excellent shell fish – Irish scallops, mussels and cockles. Although salmon is generally associated with Scotland, you may well be able to buy this in Ireland.

Barm brack is a fruity type of cake which is a speciality of Ireland. It is ideal for a picnic meal with fruit and cheese.

Irish Soda Bread

Sift 450g (1lb) plain flour, ½ teaspoon salt and ½ teaspoon bicarbonate of soda, then add 300ml (½ pint) buttermilk to make a soft dough. Make into one large or two smaller rounds. Mark the round or rounds with a cross on top. Put on to a lightly-floured baking sheet. Bake in the centre of a moderately hot oven, 200°C, 400°F, Gas Mark 6. Allow 25 minutes for smaller loaves or approximately 35 minutes for one larger loaf.

To vary:
a) Use self-raising flour, with ordinary milk and omit the bicarbonate of soda.
b) If you have no oven available, make 3 or 4 flatter rounds. Flatten each portion to fit into a frying pan. Pre-heat the frying pan; to test if it is the right heat, shake a little flour over the base of the pan. It should turn golden brown within 1 minute. Put the round of dough into the pan and cover this with a lid or plate. Cook steadily for 2–3 minutes then turn the loaf and cook for the same time on the other side. Turn the heat as low as possible and continue cooking the bread for another 8–10 minutes, turning once or twice.

IN SCOTLAND

If you have never eaten haggis, now is your great opportunity. This savoury blending of meat with oatmeal and flavourings provides a most appetizing meal. Haggis is bought from butchers, and simmered in water for about an hour; do not let the water boil too quickly, otherwise you will break the skin. The traditional accompaniment is mashed turnips or swedes.

There are no better smoked haddocks anywhere than in Scotland, the home of Finnan Haddie; you will also find Arbroath Smokies. Take care not to over-cook these delicious little haddock, for the method of smoking means they are virtually cooked. Just steam, bake or grill for a very short time, keeping them well basted with butter if grilling or baking. If you can afford it, try the really superb Scotch salmon. I have given a simple way of cooking this on page 44. Scottish herrings are magnificent, if simply coated in oatmeal then fried in butter.

The traditional Scottish baps are a beautiful soft roll, which makes a perfect breakfast bread. Scottish oatcakes are ideal to serve with cheese or main dishes. Small bakers may well have *real* shortbread, Dundee cake and Forfar bridies, a type of beef pasty or turnover.

Scottish cheeses have become very much more readily available throughout Britain, and farmers and dairymen have developed some interesting varieties. One of my favourites is Caboc, a soft, rich cream cheese coated with oatmeal.

In the game season you may be able to buy grouse or pheasant (see recipe on page 119).

You may be a little disappointed with the small selection of vegetables in outlying areas of Scotland. But the soft fruit, raspberries in particular, are probably the finest you will ever see. They tend to ripen a little later in the year than further south, and are a treat for holiday-makers in late August and September.

IN WALES

You will probably have heard of laver bread, the seaweed that is found around the shores of South Wales. Its other name is sea-spinach, which makes it sound more appetizing; this is a better description, for it is not in the least like bread – in fact enthusiasts claim it has a faint caviar flavour. If you gather it yourself it must be washed and washed again, until all traces of sand and grit have gone, then boiled in water for about 6 hours. It is then ready to use. You may be able to buy it ready-prepared to this stage.

The simplest way to cook laver bread (*bara lawr*) is to blend it with a good sprinkling of fine oatmeal, shape it into small cakes, then fry these with bacon. I like to squeeze lemon over the cakes when they are cooked.

Welsh lamb, and the more mature mutton, is some of the finest in Britain – long, slowish cooking gives mutton a moist texture. Follow the recipe on page 87. If lucky you may find katt pies – small pies filled with mutton, sweetened with brown sugar and currants.

In bakers' shops you will find Welsh cakes, small round or triangular fruit cakes. A recipe for these follows. They are cooked on a griddle (called a bakestone in Wales). You can, however, cook them in a frying pan. Bara brith is a fairly rich fruit bread, which can be eaten as a cake, that is still available in good shops.

The south coast of Wales produces excellent oysters, as well as other shell-fish. Do make sure they are fresh when you buy them. There is a recipe for shellfish soup on page 41; this is a real luxury dish if made with oysters.

Every part of Britain produces good British sausages, but if you are in Glamorgan ask for the special sausages of that area. They are made with cheese, instead of meat, and are excellent fried with bacon. They are also particularly good cold.

Welsh Cakes

Rub 100g (4oz) butter into 225g (8oz) self-raising flour, add 100g (4oz) sugar, 100g (4oz) dried fruit, 1 egg and milk to bind to a rolling consistency. Roll or pat until about 1cm (½in) thick and cut into triangles or rounds. Grease and heat a heavy frying pan or bakestone. To test shake on a little flour; it should turn golden in 1 minute. Cook the cakes for 2 minutes, turn, cook for 2 minutes, lower the heat and cook for 6–8 minutes. *Makes about 12.*

MAKE IT EASY

Throughout this book I have concentrated on those recipes that make the best use of foods available and give the holiday-maker the most interesting dishes with the minimum of effort.

These recipes would be equally suitable for holidays at home, or when travelling in Britain. There are additional ideas in this section for particularly easy ways to prepare basic foods.

PACK A GOOD STARTER

The following recipes are easy to pack and make all your picnic meals special – at home or abroad. The ingredients are easy to obtain in most countries.

Asparagus in Lemon Sauce

Drain canned asparagus and pack carefully in a long polythene box so the tips are not damaged. Blend your favourite mayonnaise with plenty of lemon juice to flavour, spoon over the asparagus and top with chopped parsley. Serve this with crusty French bread.

Avocado and Grapefruit Cocktail

First squeeze the juice of a lemon and blend this with a little salt, pepper and about 1 tablespoon oil. Cut the segments from 2 large grapefruit or drain a can of grapefruit segments. Skin, halve and slice 2 ripe avocados and blend with the grapefruit and dressing. If using fresh grapefruit, add a little sugar if you feel it is necessary. Pack into a jar and seal tightly or put into a polythene box. The order of preparing this dish is important, as it prevents the avocado discolouring.

You can vary this by adding a few shelled prawns or shrimps. If you would like to turn it into a light main dish for lunch add diced Danish blue or other well-flavoured cheese. *Serves 4–6 as an hors d'oeuvre.*

Fig and Salami Canapés

Fresh, or well-drained canned, figs blend well with salami. The classic dish, of course, is to have them with Parma ham, but this is extremely expensive and salami is a good alternative. Cut rounds or squares of brown bread, spread with butter, put the salami on top and then add a halved fig. Pack in foil or boxes.

Melon in Ginger Sauce

Blend diced melon with a little chopped preserved ginger and some of the syrup from the jar; this saves having to carry sugar and ginger, and it moistens the melon.

Melons of all kinds abound in hotter climates during the summer months; if you have never sampled water-melons, with their bright pinky-red flesh, do try these. Their flesh is rather crisp, and they are one of the most refreshing of fruits especially when chilled. They make a very good dessert.

MORE MEAL STARTERS

Basque Sardines

Use cooked fresh sardines if possible. Fry or grill these in a little oil. Skin, halve and chop 2 good-sized tomatoes, blend with 1 tablespoon tomato purée, 1–2 tablespoons finely chopped spring or other onions, 1 crushed clove garlic or a little garlic salt. Spoon over about 450g (1lb) cooked sardines while these are hot. Serve hot with crisp French bread or allow to cool and serve with salad. When fresh sardines are not available use canned ones. *Serves 4.*

Chilled Curry Soup

Blend a large can of mulligatawny soup, 300ml (½ pint) yoghourt and 2–3 tablespoons finely chopped green peppers (discard the core and seeds). Add about 100g (4oz) shelled prawns or other shell fish. Serve very cold. *Serves 4.*

Stuffed Eggs

Hard-boil 4 eggs, crack the shells, plunge into cold water to cool; shell and halve. Put the yolks into a basin, mash well and blend with 50g (2oz) pâté and 2 tablespoons finely chopped cucumber. Pile back into the egg white cases and serve with salad. *Serves 4.*

Mushrooms au Gratin

Cook approximately 175g (6oz) button mushrooms in 50g (2oz) butter. When the mushrooms are soft, stir 150ml (¼ pint) soured cream into the pan together with 2 tablespoons mayonnaise and a good shake of salt and pepper. Put into a flame-proof dish and top with thinly sliced cheese. Heat in the oven or under the grill until the cheese melts. *Serves 4.*

Shell fish Cream

This is a pleasant change from the familiar prawn cocktail. You can use any shell fish, in fact a good mixture of cooked cockles, mussels, prawns, shrimps and crabmeat would be ideal. Canned or frozen shell fish could be used. Do not add any salt with canned prawns as they are already salted. Blend about 225g (8oz) prepared shell fish with 150ml (¼ pint) yoghourt, 2–3 tablespoons mayonnaise, 1 tablespoon lemon juice or white wine vinegar, 2 tablespoons horseradish cream and a little salt and pepper.

Peel and then finely dice about a quarter of a medium-sized cucumber, add this to the fish mixture. Serve on shredded lettuce and garnish with sliced cucumber and tomatoes. *Serves 4–6.*

SIMPLE SOUPS

All these give 4 servings.

Tomato and Red Pepper Soup

Peel and chop 2 onions and 1–2 cloves of garlic; if you have no fresh garlic, flavour the soup with garlic salt. Chop finely 450g (1lb) fresh or canned, drained tomatoes. Dice 2 fresh red peppers, discarding the core and seeds, or use 2–3 canned red peppers. Heat 50g (2oz) butter or margarine in a saucepan, add the onions and garlic, cook for several minutes, add the tomatoes and peppers together with 600ml (1 pint) water, or use the liquid from canned tomatoes plus water to give this amount. Simmer for 15 minutes, add salt and pepper to taste. Stir 150ml (¼ pint) yoghourt into the soup and serve. This soup (minus the yoghourt) freezes well for 6 months. Add the yoghourt when reheating.

Golden Soup

Peel and coarsely grate 225g (8oz) carrots. Put into a pan with 600ml (1 pint) water, 1 chicken stock cube and a little salt and pepper. Bring the liquid to the boil, lower the heat and simmer for 3 minutes only: the carrots should retain their slight crispness. Blend 2 egg yolks with 150ml (¼ pint) cream (single or double) or unsweetened evaporated milk, whisk into the hot liquid and simmer gently for 2–3 minutes. Add 50–100g (2–4oz) grated cheese; do not cook again, but serve at once. This soup is better freshly made. It can be varied in many ways: add peeled and grated celeriac (celery root) or Jerusalem artichokes.

Mustard Soup

This soup is a good opportunity for you to try one of the milder French mustards. Dijon or Meaux are my particular favourites in this soup, which is really an adaptation of a mustard sauce. Blend 1 tablespoon cornflour or 2 tablespoons flour with 300ml (½ pint) milk. Put into a saucepan, adding 450ml (¾ pint) water plus 1 chicken stock cube, salt and pepper to taste, and 2–3 tablespoons French mustard. Stir as the liquid comes to the boil and continue stirring until it thickens very slightly. Beat 2 egg yolks with 150ml (¼ pint) single or double cream or unsweetened evaporated milk or top of the milk, whisk into the soup and simmer for 2–3 minutes.

If you have any spring onions, snip some of the green stalks into the soup just before serving. This soup should be freshly made.

FRYING FISH

There are many excellent dishes based on fried fish, which cut out the stages of coating the fish in egg and crumbs, or batter, or frying in a lot of fat.

These recipes are suitable for most white fish. Trout, mackerel or herrings can be substituted where indicated. Unless stated otherwise, the recipes serve 4 people.

Fish Meunière

If cooking 4 portions of white fish or 4 unsmoked trout heat 75g (3oz) butter in the frying pan, fry the fish until tender, then put on to plates. Heat the butter left in the pan until it darkens slightly. Add about 1 tablespoon lemon juice or white wine vinegar to the golden brown butter with a pinch of salt, shake of pepper and any chopped herbs you have, for example parsley, dill, fennel or tarragon. Spoon over the fish.

To vary: If you like the fish to have a slightly crisp outside dust it with a little flour, or cornflour, before cooking. A few capers can be added to the sauce.

Canary Seafood

This can be made with just one kind of fish, but it is very good if you have several varieties: cod or haddock, plaice, sole or skate, and shelled prawns. Allow one peeled banana per person. Fry fish in butter or margarine until nearly cooked, then add the bananas and fry until the fish is tender. Serve with a really crisp green salad.

Fish in Paprika Sauce

Fry 4 portions of white fish in 50g (2oz) butter or margarine until just tender. Add 300ml (½ pint) yoghourt, 1–2 teaspoons paprika, a squeeze of lemon juice and a little salt and pepper. Heat in the frying pan with the fish for several minutes. Serve with lots of sliced cucumber.

Mackerel in Mustard Sauce

Cut the heads from 4 good-sized mackerel, split the fish and remove the back bones. Spread a little French mustard inside each mackerel. Fry the mackerel in 50g (2oz) butter or margarine until tender. Blend 1–2 teaspoons French mustard with 300ml (½ pint) yoghourt and ¼–½ diced cucumber. Lift the fish on to plates and top with the cold yoghourt mixture. Serve with watercress if this is available.

Herring and fresh trout are equally good served in this way.

CHEESE SNACKS

These should all be served freshly made. The ingredients in the recipes cover four large slices of buttered toasted bread.

Jamaican Toasts

Top the hot toast with sliced bananas and a generous layer of grated cheese. Heat quickly under the grill.

Sardine Savoury

Bone and mash sardines from one large can with salt, pepper and a little lemon juice. Spread on hot toast, top with 75g (3oz) grated cheese and heat under grill.

Soufflé Ham Toasts

Blend 2 egg yolks, 75–100g (3–4oz) chopped cooked ham, 175g (6oz) grated cheese, ½–1 teaspoon made mustard, 25g (1oz) butter and 1 tablespoon milk. Fold in the 2 stiffly whisked egg whites. Spread over the hot toast and grill *steadily* until well risen and golden brown.

Potato and Celery Rarebit

Blend together 175g (6oz) soft mashed potatoes*, 175g (6oz) grated cheese and ½ teaspoon made mustard. Top the hot toast with heated and well drained canned celery hearts. Spread the rarebit mixture over the top and grill steadily.
*Instant dehydrated potato could be used.

EGG DISHES

Eggs are a wonderful food for holidays. They can be used as the basis for many meals, they cook quickly and blend with most ingredients.
The recipes give 2 large or 4 smaller portions.

Crisp-crust Omelette

Dice 2 slices of bread; heat 50g (2oz) butter in the pan, fry the bread until crisp and golden brown. Check there is enough butter; you may be using an unknown omelette or frying pan that has had indifferent care and in which food is inclined to stick. If doubtful, add another 25g (1oz) butter, and heat this.
Beat 4–5 eggs with a good pinch of salt and pepper and two tablespoons water. Pour over the bread, allow to cook, tilting the pan backwards and forwards so the liquid egg flows to the sides of the pan and sets quickly. Fold the omelette and serve.
This omelette can be varied in many ways. Chopped bacon and sliced, cooked potatoes can be fried with the bread.

Egg and Cheese Medley

Grate about 50g (2oz) of a good cooking cheese; thinly slice about 100g (4oz) of the same cheese. Put the sliced cheese into a shallow casserole; add a well-drained can of asparagus tips. Break 4 eggs on to the cheese and asparagus, add a pinch of salt, shake of pepper, 2–3 tablespoons single cream or top of the milk and the grated cheese. Bake for about 15 minutes just above the centre of a moderate oven, 190°C, 375°F, Gas Mark 5, until the eggs are set. Serve with crusty fresh bread.

Uitsmijter

The simple Dutch snack makes slices of cold meat much more interesting. Cut 4 fairly thick slices of fresh bread, spread with butter and top with slices of cooked ham, beef or other meat. Fry eggs in hot butter, place on top of the meat and serve with salad.

Speedy Fritters

Blend 2 eggs, 50g (2oz) self-raising flour or plain flour with ½ teaspoon baking powder, a pinch of salt, pepper and 1 teaspoon made mustard. Lastly add 50g (2oz) grated cheese or chopped cooked ham, or a mixture of the two. Heat 50g (2oz) fat in a frying pan. Drop spoonfuls of the mixture into the hot fat and fry for 2 minutes on each side.

Serve hot or cold with salad.

Cheese-filled Peppers

Grate 100g (4oz) any firm cheese and add to 225g (8oz) cream or cottage cheese, together with 1 tablespoon chopped parsley, 1 tablespoon chopped chives or grated onion, a little lemon juice, salt and pepper and a few drops of milk to bind. Chop a small red pepper finely, discarding the core and seeds. Blend the chopped pepper with the cheese mixture. Remove the core and seeds from 4 green peppers, but keep the shells intact. Trim the tops level, finely chop the trimmings, and add to the cheese mixture. Fill the green pepper shells with the cheese mixture.

Chill for a while if possible, so the filling becomes quite firm, then cut across into slices and serve on crispbread or buttered bread. *Serves 4–6.*

Freezing: Frozen peppers cannot be used for this, they must be fresh and crisp.

PAN-COOKED VEGETABLES

The following recipes are for quick, hot vegetable dishes. Use made-up instant potatoes if desired. Recipes are for 4 portions.

Colcannon

Peel and chop an onion. Heat 50g (2oz) butter in a strong frying pan. Cook the onion for several minutes. Add about 225g (8oz) shredded cooked cabbage, 450g (1lb) mashed potatoes, several tablespoons of cream, or top of the milk, and a little salt and pepper. Heat thoroughly and serve.

Paprika Mushrooms

Wash and cut about 350g (12oz) large mushrooms into thick slices, or leave small mushrooms whole. Fry steadily in 50–75g (2–3oz) butter or margarine for 5–6 minutes. Add 150ml (¼ pint) yoghourt and 1–2 teaspoons paprika and stir to blend with the mushrooms, season well and serve.

Sliced cucumber or diced cooked beetroot can also be cooked in this way.

Potato Cakes

Blend together approximately 225g (8oz) mashed potatoes, 50g (2oz) self-raising flour, or plain flour and ½ teaspoon baking powder. Test the consistency; it should be possible to roll it out. If too dry, add a little milk, if too wet knead on a well-floured board. Roll out to approximately 0·5cm (¼in) in thickness. Cut into rounds. Grease, then heat a frying pan. Cook the cakes until brown on each side. Serve with savoury dishes, or topped with brown sugar as a sweet dish.

Potato Pancakes

Peel 4 good-sized potatoes and then grate, using the coarse side of the grater. Put this into a basin, add 1 egg, salt, pepper and enough flour to make a thick batter (about 50g (2oz)). Mix well. Heat a little fat in the frying pan; drop spoonfuls of the mixture in the fat, fry steadily, allowing about 3 minutes on each side, then drain and serve.

Ratatouille

Slice an aubergine and 2 courgettes (zucchini) – none of these needs peeling. Chop a green pepper, discarding the core and seeds, and several skinned tomatoes. Peel and chop 1–2 onions and 1–2 cloves of garlic. Heat 2–3 tablespoons oil and fry the vegetables gently, stirring for the first 5 minutes. Put a plate or lid over the frying pan so the liquid from the vegetables does not evaporate. Simmer for 20–25 minutes.

COOKING JACKET POTATOES

Old potatoes are often baked in their skins (jackets), but new potatoes are also delicious cooked in this way.

If you have no oven, cook the potatoes in the minimum of salted water in a tightly covered saucepan.

When baking potatoes in their jackets, wash, dry, prick the skins, then rub with a little butter or oil to encourage the skins to crisp.

Cook extra potatoes to serve in salads. Cooking potatoes in their jackets preserves all their flavour and vitamins. Top the cooked potatoes with butter or cottage cheese or soured cream.

Good-sized jacket potatoes will take about 1–1¼ hours in the centre of a moderate to moderately hot oven, 190–200°C, 375–400°F, Gas Mark 5–6; and although new potatoes are much smaller they do take about 50 minutes.

Old potatoes can be stuffed in many ways to form delicious supper dishes; some ideas are given below. Cut each potato in half, scoop out the pulp, mash with butter, a little salt and pepper and proceed as the suggestions given.

Barbecue

To 4 large potatoes allow 4 rashers bacon, 2 dessert apples, 4 cooked or Frankfurter sausages. De-rind and dice the bacon, dice the apples, (core, but there is no need to peel them), slice the sausages. Fry the food in about 25g (1oz) butter, add a sprinkling of sugar, Worcestershire sauce and mustard to taste. Pile the mashed potato back into the jacket halves. Hollow out the centre of each into a nest shape and fill with the bacon mixture. Reheat in the oven for a few minutes if necessary.

Ploughman's Delight

Blend the mashed potato with grated cheese and sweet chutney or pickle – return to the jacket halves and reheat if necessary.

Potatoes Provençale

Pile the mashed potato carefully back into the jacket halves. Form the mashed potato into nest shapes in the potato cases. Fill the hollows with canned or home-made ratatouille (see page 118), then reheat if necessary.

Potato and Seafood

Heat a can of thick fish soup while the potatoes cook, adding extra shelled shrimps or prawns. Hollow out the mashed potatoes in the potato skins. Fill the hollows with the fish mixture. For a delicious flavour, add a little chopped fennel and fennel leaves to the filling. Reheat if necessary.

More Savoury Ideas

Left-over cooked ham, chicken, corned beef, canned kidneys, sliced sausages or diced cheese can all be mixed with the mashed potato before piling back into the jacket halves. Reheat if necessary.

GAME

Pheasant Casserole

You may be on holiday in the game season and be able to buy a pheasant – plucked and ready for cooking. This casserole recipe is equally good for a young pheasant or a more mature bird. A really plump pheasant will serve up to 4 people.

Wash and dry the pheasant and put it into a casserole. De-rind and chop 3–4 bacon rashers and put round the pheasant. Spread 50g (2oz) butter over the pheasant, but do not cover the casserole. Place this in the centre of a hot oven, 220°C, 425°F, Gas Mark 7 and leave for about 15 minutes or until the bird begins to colour. Meanwhile, prepare a bunch of spring onions, discarding the stalks; add the onions, 300ml (½ pint) dry cider or white wine, a little salt and pepper, a small can of stoned cherries (optional) and a few olives to the pheasant. Cover the casserole with a lid or foil. If cooking a young pheasant reduce the heat to moderate, 190°C, 375°F, Gas Mark 5 and cook for another 45 minutes, or until tender. If cooking an older bird reduce the heat to very moderate, 160°C, 325°F, Gas Mark 3 and leave for approximately 1½ hours.Serve with peas or a salad.

To vary: Other game birds, chicken, guinea fowl or young rabbit can be cooked like a pheasant.

Use fresh cherries in place of canned ones.

Freezing: The casserole freezes well.

MEAT
DISHES FOR CAMPERS

The dishes which follow use just one pan, either a saucepan or a deep frying pan. The quantities are for 4 people.

Curried Beef

Put a can of curry sauce, diluted if necessary according to the directions on the can, into a saucepan. Add the well washed bulbs from a small bunch of spring onions and 1 peeled and diced dessert apple. Cover the pan and simmer for 5–6 minutes, then add a 350g (12oz) can of corned beef, which should be neatly diced. Heat for 5 minutes.

Chicken Fricassée

Use either canned or packet mushroom soup for the basis of the sauce. You need approximately 600ml (1 pint) for 4 people. Place 4 chicken joints in the soup in a saucepan and simmer for nearly 15 minutes. Add a small can of well-drained peas (or use a packet of frozen peas) and a small can or packet of sweetcorn. Continue simmering for another 10–15 minutes until the chicken is very tender. Add salt and pepper to taste. Serve with wedges of lemon, potato crisps and lettuce to make a contrasting texture.

Ham Barbecue

Use either 350g (12oz) canned ham or thickly-sliced fresh ham for this recipe. Cut the ham into neat dice. Tip a 425g (15oz) can tomatoes into a saucepan, add 1 tablespoon vinegar, 1 tablespoon cooking oil, 1 tablespoon sugar (brown, if available), ½ tablespoon made English mustard or French mustard and 1 teaspoon Worcestershire sauce. Heat for 10 minutes very gently; stir well to break up the tomatoes, add a good shake of pepper, but only a little salt if the ham is well salted. Put the ham into the sauce and heat. Serve with watercress and lettuce.

Camper's Steak Diane

Peel and grate 2 medium onions. Heat 50g (2oz) butter plus 1 tablespoon oil in a pan. Fry the onions for 2–3 minutes, then add 4 portions of steak, cook for a few minutes, add about 150ml (¼ pint) cider or white wine plus ½–1 tablespoon Worcestershire sauce, a little salt and pepper and 1 tablespoon chopped parsley, if available. Simmer until cooked to personal taste. If it is difficult to fit the pieces of steak into the pan, cut them into fingers.
Serve with a mixed salad.

EASY WAYS TO SERVE CHICKEN

The following recipes give some quick and easy suggestions for serving chicken. You can either roast a chicken or buy a ready-cooked chicken and just warm this in the oven. If you have no oven, joint the chicken first, or buy chicken joints. Fry steadily in a frying pan in fat or oil until tender. A cooked chicken can be heated through in a small amount of fat. Prepare the sauce or accompaniments while the chicken heats. These sauces are made in minutes.

Arabian Chicken

Put 2 tablespoons honey, 25g (1oz) butter, the juice of a large orange (or about 3 tablespoons bottled orange juice) into a saucepan and add 2 tablespoons chopped preserved ginger. If you have no ginger, add 1 teaspoon ground ginger. Open a can of mandarin oranges, drain off the syrup and blend this with 1½ teaspoons cornflour; add to the ingredients in the saucepan and stir over a low heat until the mixture thickens and is clear. Add the mandarin oranges and continue cooking for 2–3 minutes. Spoon over the chicken. Serve with a crisp green salad. *Serves 4–6.*

Devilled Chicken

Chop 2 large onions or use the equivalent in dried onion. Heat 25g (1oz) fat in a pan and fry the onions until tender. Add a can of tomato soup with 1 teaspoon curry powder, 1–2 teaspoons Worcestershire sauce and a pinch of cayenne pepper. Heat for a short time. Serve the chicken with the sauce and boiled rice. *Serves 4–6.*

Paprika Chicken

Put 25g (1oz) butter into a pan, add 300ml (½ pint) yoghourt, 2–3 teaspoons paprika, salt and pepper and 1 teaspoon French or made English mustard. Heat gently, stirring well. Serve the chicken with the sauce and boiled rice. *Serves 4–6.*

Supreme of Chicken

Put the yolks of 3 eggs, 1 tablespoon lemon juice, 300ml (½ pint) water, 1 chicken stock cube and 150ml (¼ pint) single cream into a basin over hot water. Stir until thickened, then add salt and pepper to taste. For this dish carve just the chicken breast, place in the sauce and carefully heat through. Serve with boiled rice. *Serves 4–6.*

FRUIT DESSERTS IN MINUTES

Although fresh fruit is an ideal dessert, many people feel a meal is incomplete without a 'proper' dessert. The following suggestions are all possible with the most limited cooking equipment. The dishes serve 4.

Blushing Apples

Put 300ml (½ pint) water, 50g (2oz) sugar and 2–3 tablespoons redcurrant jelly into a saucepan or deep frying pan. Stir until the sugar has dissolved. Peel 4–6 dessert apples and put them into the liquid; simmer for about 10 minutes, turning the apples around as they cook, until they are pale pink. Serve hot or cold.

Pears could be used instead of apples.

The apples can be frozen in the syrup, but are really nicer freshly cooked.

Soufflé Berries

You may have egg whites left after using the yolks in other recipes. These will give a very easy and delicious soufflé. Crush about 350g (12oz) ripe strawberries, raspberries, red or blackcurrants. Blend with 50–75g (2–3oz) sugar. Whisk 4 egg whites until stiff and fold into the berry mixture. Spoon into an ovenproof dish and bake in the centre of a moderately hot oven, 200°C, 400°F, Gas Mark 6 for 20–25 minutes until well risen. Serve at once with cream or ice cream.

This cannot be frozen, but it is an excellent way of using defrosted frozen fruit.

Yoghourt and Banana Caramel

Put 25g (1oz) butter and 3 tablespoons sugar, preferably brown, into a frying pan. Stir over a low heat until the sugar begins to turn a darker brown. Add 4 large or 8 small peeled bananas and roll round in the sugar mixture. Add 300ml (½ pint) plain or orange-flavoured yoghourt and stir over a low heat for about 5 minutes. Serve hot.

This should be freshly cooked.

RUN OUT OF BREAD!!

If you have been travelling and have had no time to buy bread, these cobs and rusks are very easy to make.

Cobs

Preheat the oven at 220°C, 425°F, Gas Mark 7. Blend 225g (8oz) self-raising flour and a pinch of salt. Rub in a small knob of butter or margarine (about 15g (½oz)) then bind the dough with 150ml (¼ pint) milk. Divide the mixture into about 8 portions, roll in balls with floured fingers and bake for about 10 minutes above the centre of the oven. Eat when fresh. *Makes 8.*

Suffolk Rusks

Make the dough as above, but use slightly less milk to give a dough which can be rolled out. Roll out on a lightly floured surface – if you have no rolling pin then use an empty bottle or jar or just pat out the dough until about 1·5cm (¾in) in thickness. Cut into rounds (the rim of a tumbler can be used). Put on to a baking sheet and bake for about 10–12 minutes in a moderate oven, 180°C, 350°F, Gas Mark 4. By this time the rusks will be sufficiently set to handle. Cool for a few minutes, then lift the first round from the tray and split horizontally, to give two thinner rounds. Place the cut side downwards on to the baking sheet, lower the heat slightly and continue cooking for another 15–20 minutes until firm and crisp. Cool, then pack into an airtight tin. *Makes 16–18.*